THE NUREMBERG TRIALS

THE NUREMBERG TRIALS

THE NAZIS AND THEIR CRIMES AGAINST HUMANITY

PAUL ROLAND

CHARTWELL
BOOKS, INC.

This edition printed in 2010 by
CHARTWELL BOOKS, INC.
A Division of **BOOK SALES, INC.**
276 Fifth Avenue Suite 206
New York, New York 10001 USA

Copyright © 2010 Arcturus Publishing Limited
26/27 Bickels Yard, 151–153 Bermondsey Street,
London SE1 3HA

ISBN-13: 978-0-7858-2607-1
ISBN-10: 0-7858-2607-6
AD001217EN

Printed in China

Contents

Introduction

The Nuremberg War Crimes Trials began on 20 November 1945 and ended on 13 April 1949. At the first trial, twenty-four leading Nazis were indicted, but only 21 defendants made an appearance. On 9 December 1946, 12 subsequent trials of 'lesser war criminals' were held by the Americans. A summary of these hearings will be found in the final chapter.

Why another book about the Nuremberg War Crimes Trials? It is true that the story has been re-told many times, but it bears repetition because with the passing of time the Nazis have assumed an almost mythic status in the minds of those who did not experience the war, or the horrors of the concentration camps. There is a very real danger that for subsequent generations they will be reduced to two-dimensional villains – no more real than the sinister SS caricatures in the Indiana Jones films.

Of more importance, though, is the fact that the lessons of Nuremberg do not appear to have been learned. There are still those who deny the Holocaust – despite the fact that Holocaust denial is now a crime in many European countries including Germany – but they do so in the face of the facts that are presented in this book,

Heinrich Himmler was one of the prime architects of the Holocaust and oversaw the concentration camp system. The first to be opened in March 1933 was Dachau, which he is here seen inspecting with other SS officers.

where the personal testimonies of eyewitnesses are verified by the words of the accused themselves.

Another reason why I felt compelled to write this account was that I have managed to unearth several personal recollections that to the best of my knowledge have never been published in book form. They are not of great length, nor even of great significance from a historical point of view, but they reveal certain aspects of the trials, and the personalities involved, that are not generally known. But of more importance, they underline the impression that all of the characters in this human catastrophe were quite ordinary people,

Adolf Hitler meets his adoring public. He dreamed of a Europe ruled solely by the Ayrian master-race.

who were living through extraordinary times. And that includes the defendants.

The Nazis continue to hold a morbid fascination for many people. However, when they were stripped of their Satanic symbolism, and dispossessed of the power over life and death that fed their fanatical arrogance, Hermann Goering, Albert Speer, Joachim von Ribbentrop and the rest of the Hitler gang were reduced to their essence – which in many cases was as pitiable as it was disturbing. Here was the 'banality of evil' laid bare. Hitler's followers were the very embodiment of *Untermenschen* (the subhumans of Aryan master race mythology), who blindly obeyed immoral orders without recourse to their own conscience. They were men of diverse backgrounds – able military leaders, petty bureaucrats and mechanical functionaries. Some of them should have known better but they all willingly sold their souls to bring a madman's nightmares to reality, feeding his neuroses and propagating his paranoid racist propaganda without considering the inevitable consequences of their actions. Deprived of the pretence of Teutonic heroism, and denied the ritual staging of their Wagnerian party rallies, the Nuremberg defendants were finally forced to face the sordid reality of the damage that their racist ideology and extreme nationalism had wrought upon the world.

It is a disquieting fact that we tend to find villains more interesting than their victims – in fiction and in reality – but the Nuremberg Trials revealed that in real life criminals and murderers are invariably colourless individuals, who lack personality as well as compassion and conscience. It is their victims who frequently display courage and endurance beyond normal human experience. And that aspect of human nature has, I hope, been brought out in this account of the trials. For the final reason for writing this account was to give voice to the survivors of Nazi atrocities – those who had witnessed unimaginable horrors but had still found the courage to continue with their lives. Women such as Clara Greenbaum…

The Nightmare Revealed

'... Here over an acre of ground lay dead and dying people. You could not see which was which... The living lay with their heads against the corpses and around them moved the awful, ghostly procession of emaciated, aimless people, with nothing to do and with no hope of life, unable to move out of your way, unable to look at the terrible sights around them... Babies had been born here, tiny wizened things that could not live... A mother, driven mad, screamed at a British sentry to give her milk for her child, and thrust the tiny mite into his arms, then ran off, crying terribly. He opened the bundle and found the baby had been dead for days. This day at Belsen was the most horrible of my life.'

RICHARD DIMBLEBY, BBC CORRESPONDENT

On the morning of 15 April 1945, Clara Greenbaum woke from an uneasy sleep to the realization that her recurring nightmare had no end. She was still incarcerated in the notorious Nazi slave labour camp at Belsen in northwestern Germany, where an estimated 100,000 prisoners, half of them Russian prisoners of war, had died since its inception in 1943. Clara and her two children – Hannah aged seven and Adam, who was not yet four – were just three of some 60,000 inmates who had miraculously survived starvation, summary execution and the typhus epidemic. Typhus alone had claimed the lives of up to 35,000 prisoners in the first few months of 1945. But no less of a hazard was the daily brutality meted out by the sadistic SS guards, who beat the prisoners unmercifully and frequently shot them at random for 'target practice'.

The Germans were not the only oppressors in that man-made hell on earth. There were also the hated *Kapos*, the trustees who burst into the barracks each morning. They barked out orders and cursed and banged on the bunks with their sticks. It would surely be only a few minutes before their regular *Kapo* came in and the silence of the morning was shattered. Clara was always torn between allowing the children to rest and waking them to save them from being startled from their slumber. If she relented and let them sleep they would wake up crying and she would have to comfort them while getting them ready for roll call. It was all part of the daily ritual of the camp. She had also created her own rituals, feeling that some form of routine would enable her to keep her sanity. These included keeping a record of the number of days that had passed since her arrest on suspicion of being a member of the French underground. To date she had survived 818 days of imprisonment – two and a half years of privation and hard labour – with no more than a bowl of watered-down soup and a slice of bread each day to sustain a life that had no value to the Nazis other than as a unit of labour. Snapping out of her reverie she checked the children who slept in the bunk behind her, to see if they had survived the night. In addition to her own children, she had adopted those whose mothers had died. At any one time there might be up to five children crowded into that one cot. Then she would check the two women with whom she shared her bunk. If one or both had died in the night she would search the corpse for a scrap of food that might have been hidden away, or an item of clothing that could keep her warm in the bitter weather. The only chance of acquiring a new pair of socks or a scarf was to take it from a dead body. Concentration camp inmates did not receive Red Cross parcels.

The next thing she remembered was waking up again. Incredibly she had fallen asleep and her dreams had not been disturbed by the *Kapo*. Her first thought was that she was dead. There was no other explanation for the fact that the *Kapo* had not woken her. Then she was overwhelmed by fear. Being late for assembly was a punishable offence. Inmates had been publicly hanged for less. Turning over she saw that her children were still sleeping. Her anxiety intensified, for they too would be punished. Sitting up she saw that many of her fellow inmates were awake. Some were even standing in the aisle between the bunks. They were speaking to each other in whispers. What was going on? The only explanation that made any sense was that the

One of the mass graves at Belsen concentration camp, which housed political prisoners and Russian prisoners of war. Most of the inmates died of malnutrition and ill-treatment. The camp was liberated by the British 11th Armoured Division on 15 April 1945. They found 60,000 prisoners seriously ill but still alive.

Kapos had deliberately let them sleep so they would have an excuse to punish them all.

For two or three hours Clara remained rigid with terror, her fists clenched. She was unable to think because she feared that at any moment the guards would burst in, their dogs straining at the leash, firing their guns into the ceiling as they rounded up the prisoners like cattle for slaughter. But nothing happened. Then the suffocating silence was broken by a terrible sound as a hysterical woman stumbled screaming towards the door, threw it open and disappeared outside, slamming it shut behind her. The tension had been too much. Her mind had given way. Her screams grew fainter. Everyone waited for the sound of a shot, but all was silence. The door opened again and another desperate woman, who could only crawl, went out into the unknown. She was followed by yet another, who left the door open, allowing a stream of light to illuminate the dormitory. Clara's children crawled into her bunk, the first time they had done so in two years. They buried their haunted faces in her body, breathing hard. When they had attempted to join their mother on an earlier occasion the two women she shared her bunk with had screamed at them to go back, because there was no room. Now they did not object. They knew something momentous was happening, something they dared not articulate, nor believe. Before long the entire room had emptied. Only Clara and the children remained cowering on the bunk. It was thirst that finally forced her to act. She took Hannah and Adam by the hand and approached the door, with the other children trailing closely behind.

Outside, it was an overcast day. It had rained during the night and Clara hoped there might be some water in the ditch near the assembly area to quench her thirst. When she reached it she was astounded to see thousands of prisoners converging on the square from all corners of the camp. Many were walking unsteadily and in a daze. The dirty, tattered rags that fluttered around their emaciated frames made them look like living scarecrows. Those who were too exhausted or too ill to walk unaided were being helped by their friends, while some crawled on all fours. Large numbers of prisoners lay dying or dead where only yesterday they had been forced to stand to attention. The contrast was too surreal for Clara to take in at first. She almost wished for order to return, because she was so conditioned by those who held the power of life and death in this accursed place. Looking up she noticed that the guard towers were empty. In fact, there were no guards to be seen anywhere. But if this was the day of liberation, it did not feel like it. There was no elation, only a crippling anxiety. For four hours the mass of prisoners remained on the Appellplatz, not daring to approach the unguarded gates. Many of them must have realized that they were only a few hundred metres from freedom, but they were unable to move. It was not that they were afraid that the guards would return but, as Clara later remembered, the guards were still inside them and they would remain there to the end of their lives. They were so indoctrinated that the very thought of freedom filled them with fear. It was not only their bodies that had been imprisoned and tortured beyond endurance, but their minds.

Hours passed and then the mass of people stirred. They could hear the unmistakable sound of heavy vehicles approaching from behind the low hills to the

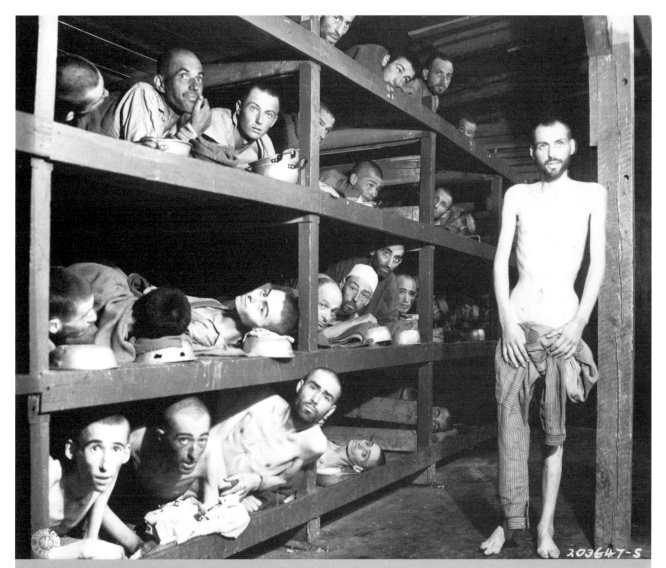

Slave labourers in the Buchenwald concentration camp near Weimar, one of the first camps to be liberated by US soldiers in April 1945. The camp's first commandant from 1937 to 1941, Karl Otto Koch, was himself imprisoned here for corruption and was tried and executed by the Nazis shortly before the camp's liberation.

north. A moment later a column of tanks and trucks appeared. The vehicles were rumbling across the ploughed fields towards the barbed wire. Panic went through the crowd like a bolt of electricity. This was it. The Germans were going to machine-gun them and then roll over their bodies to eradicate the evidence of their crimes. Then someone saw the Union Jack flying from the turret of one of the tanks. They were British! To the prisoners' amazement the column circled the camp twice before drawing up in formation at the front gates, where the vehicles' engines were turned off. Presumably they had been checking to see if any SS troops were prepared to make a final stand. And there they waited. Not a word was spoken. No orders were given. Clara estimated that as many as 500 troops were standing in complete silence, staring through the barbed wire.

Liberated women prisoners from the Bergen-Belsen concentration camp line up to be dusted with DDT (to combat insect-borne typhus) by a British soldier, May 1945.

What were they waiting for? And then one of the soldiers doubled up and retched. Another vomited and then another. So that was it. They had been staring at the inmates in disgust. Hardened soldiers were sick to their stomachs at the sight of them. At that, many prisoners turned away. They were ashamed of what they were, of what they had become.

Then some of the soldiers began throwing food over the fence and the prisoners scrambled to claim what they could. A moment later the leading tank roared into life and smashed through the gates, followed by orderly ranks of soldiers under the command of an officer. The inmates had been liberated, but Clara felt no joy. She only wanted to turn and hide. But after a few steps she was arrested by a terrible sound. It was the mourning wail of an old woman. Only it was not an old woman. It was Hannah. For the first time in three years she was crying – her convulsions were so violent that her mother feared that her small body would collapse. For three years she had kept her emotions in check, but now they had all risen to the surface and consumed her. Adam was also weeping, but in the way that a small child cries. That was the moment at which Clara's stony resolve cracked. She too fell to the ground, screaming and pounding the dirt with her fists. Everything they had seen and suffered had to be exorcized.

The survivors needed to be questioned before having their details taken for a Red Cross list, but first of all they were given soup. Clara asked for water to dilute it with because she knew that she and her children were too malnourished to drink it as it was. Even so they felt sick afterwards. Others were not so lucky. The soup was too much for their ravaged bodies and they died.

**'In the concentration camp you cannot have hope.
Only determination.'**

CLARA GREENBAUM

Soldiers' Justice

In other camps Allied officers found it difficult to maintain discipline among their men – in some cases captured SS guards were summarily executed. This was soldiers' justice, meted out by men who had seen their share of death, but who could no longer restrain themselves when confronted with the cold-blooded slaughter, or brutalization, of innocent civilians.

The bodies of more than 2,000 prisoners from other camps, who had died chiefly from starvation en route to Dachau concentration camp for extermination, filled these railroad cars when they were discovered by American soldiers at the end of April 1945.

At Dachau, near Munich, the liberators were checking the railway sidings when 2,310 corpses spilled out of a single train. It had been bringing in prisoners from other camps for execution. Most of the dead, including 83 women and 21 children, had expired from malnutrition, dehydration and suffocation – the Germans had crammed them in several hundred to a wagon. Those who had survived the journey were dragged out before being shot, beaten to death with rifle butts or torn to pieces by the guard dogs.

The corpses were so emaciated that the first American officer on the scene thought he was looking at mounds of rags. Then he realized that the pathetic bundles were human beings. He estimated that the heaviest of them could not have weighed more than sixty or seventy pounds. With considerable effort he managed to keep his composure and then he attempted to maintain discipline by ordering his men – many of whom were sobbing uncontrollably – to count the corpses. But he was too late to prevent a GI from machine-gunning a number of captured SS personnel (as many as 122 Germans died, according to some accounts) while his squad urged him on, aided by the inhuman cries of the prisoners behind the wire.

The bodies of SS guards lie just outside Dachau concentration camp where they were shot by US soldiers exercising their own form of summary justice for the atrocities they had witnessed.

But the SS were anonymous servants of the Nazi regime. Their names and their fate would be lost among the appalling statistics of a war that had claimed some 64 million victims in 27 countries, 40 million of them non-combatants. Besides, the survivors did not want revenge, they wanted justice. Someone would have to pay, and be seen to pay, for what

The tables turned. Long-term prisoners of Dachau concentration camp hurl insults at one of the SS guards they have just knocked down following the liberation of the camp by the Americans, April 1945.

the Nazi regime had done to Clara and millions like her, many of whom had simply vanished from the earth, cremated in the ovens of Auschwitz and more than a thousand other camps throughout Germany and the occupied countries. The architects of the Final Solution would have to be brought to account and the German nation must be forced to face up to its collective responsibility for giving Hitler the mandate to wage his war. There would have to be a trial.

'I never dreamed that such cruelty, bestiality, and savagery could really exist in this world... I made the visit (to Buchenwald) deliberately, in order to be in a position to give first-hand evidence of these things if ever, in the future, there develops a tendency to charge these allegations merely to "propaganda".'

GENERAL EISENHOWER

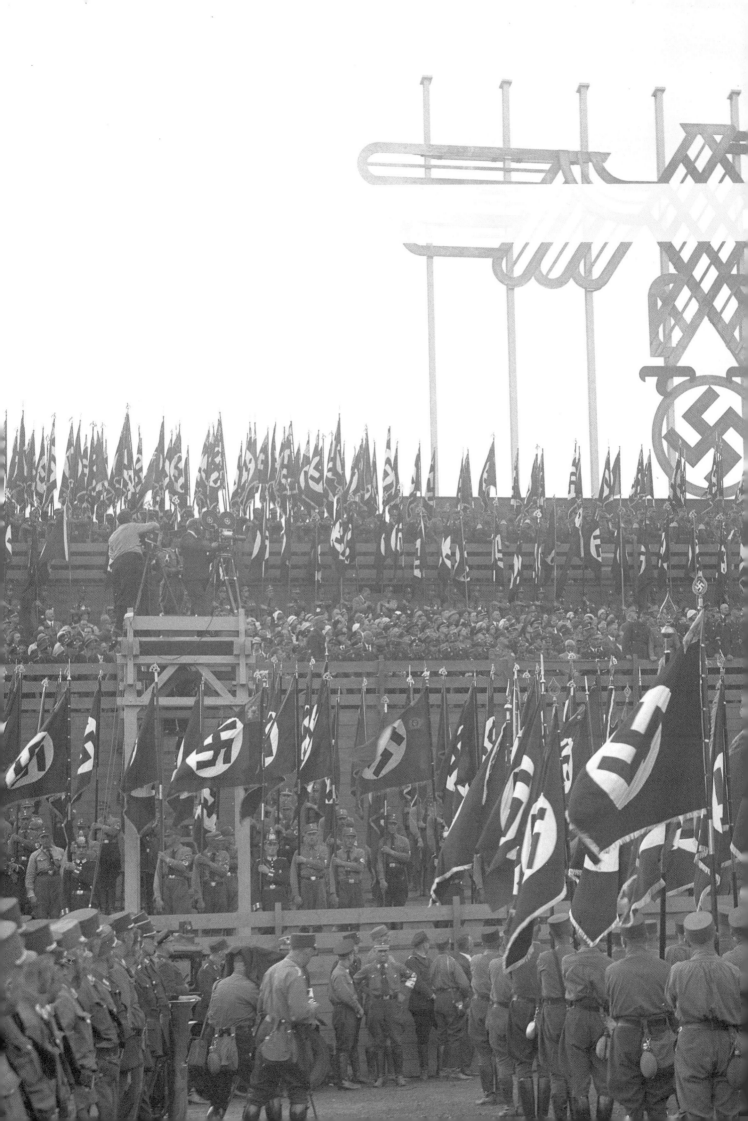

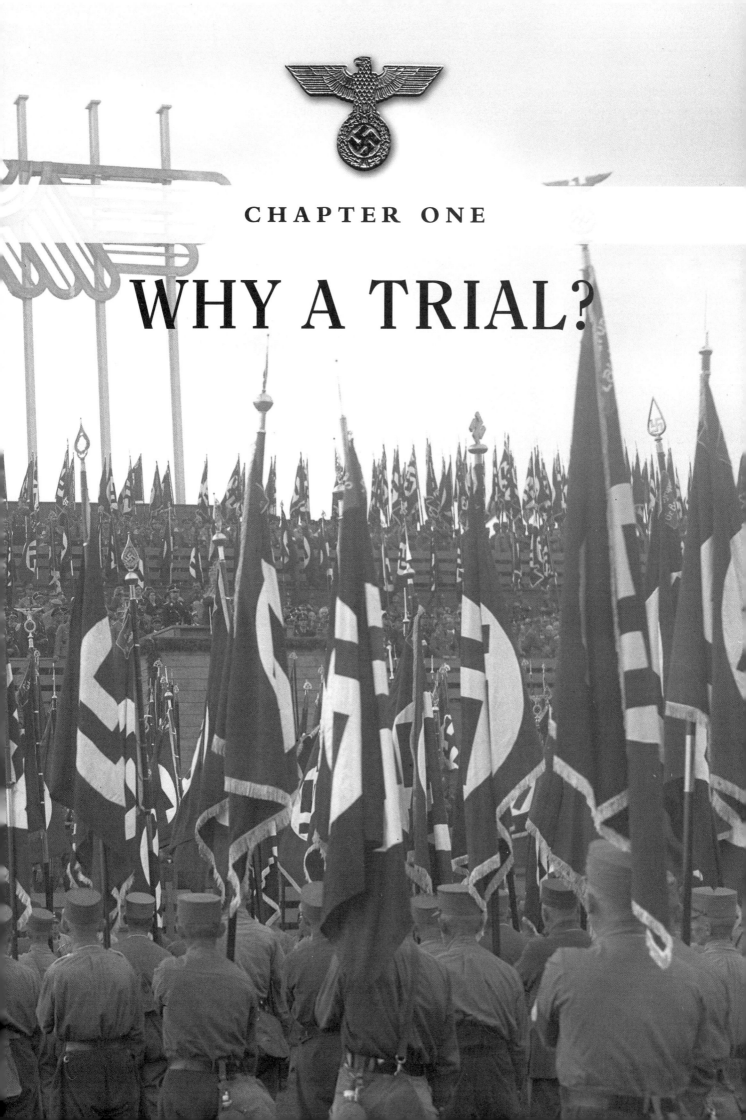

CHAPTER ONE

WHY A TRIAL?

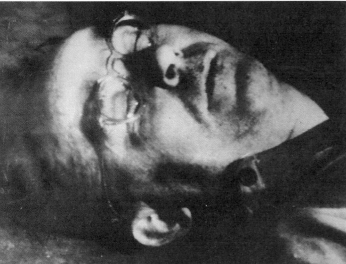

The perfect Nazi family? Joseph and Magda Goebbels and their six children (top) all died by cyanide in the **Führerbunker;** *Heinrich Himmler (above) committed suicide by cyanide capsule while in British custody.*

With the end of the Second World War in Europe in May 1945, the victorious Allies were faced with a dilemma. Nazi dictator Adolf Hitler had committed suicide in his bunker in Berlin on 30 April and two of his most notorious henchmen – his propaganda minister Joseph Goebbels and SS Reichsführer Heinrich Himmler – had followed his example. Other high-ranking Nazi officials such as Adolf Eichmann and Gestapo chief Heinrich Mueller, together with infamous instruments of the regime like Dr Josef Mengele, had fled to South America or vanished into the anonymity and rubble of the Third Reich. As a result, it would be difficult to assemble enough Nazi figureheads to fill a courtroom.

At the same time, there was an acute awareness that imposing punitive reparations on the German nation, as had been done after the First World War, might contribute to the resentment and sense of injustice on which the Nazis had feasted in their rise to power. There must be no chance of a Fascist resurgence in Germany, or of the Nazi leaders being seen as martyrs. Memories of the embarrassing Leipzig trials after the First World War were still fresh in the mind. In 1921 the Allies had allowed Germany to prosecute those of its own countrymen who were accused of war crimes, but of 900 named and arraigned only two were convicted and even they escaped house arrest shortly afterwards. One of those accused had been Field Marshal von Hindenburg, who later became president of the Weimar Republic. His vacillations made it possible for Hitler to rise to power in 1933.

The Allies decided that Germany needed to renounce its past and that the best way of achieving that end was to assist in its rebuilding, while exposing its defeated leaders as the architects of its destruction. Germany was in ruins. Its cities were flattened, its infrastructure and its industry had been decimated and its citizens had been bombed out of their homes. Many were now enduring the privations that had been experienced by the people of Warsaw, Belgrade, Leningrad and numerous other cities that had been gutted as the Nazi war machine rolled mercilessly over Europe and into Russia.

However, the Allies did not send in *Einsatzgruppen* (death squads) to murder civilians in the wake of their advancing troops, nor did they set up concentration camps, forced labour camps and death camps to exterminate 'undesirable' elements of the population while working the remainder to death.

In fact, the defeated German armed forces were held in conditions that were considerably better than those they had offered their own prisoners and they were accorded all the rights due to them under the Geneva Convention – something the Germans had cynically failed to do in many cases. Furthermore, the German people were free to rebuild their lives. Nevertheless many resented the occupying forces and they made their feelings clear. Few blamed Hitler and his gang for having brought this situation upon them and fewer still were willing to believe the stories of mass murder, even after they had been forced to view the mounds of corpses in the camps. The Mayor of Gotha and his wife hanged themselves for shame after they had visited Buchenwald, but many of their fellow townspeople simply covered their faces and hurried past the open graves. It was Allied propaganda, they told themselves. These had been political prisoners – Communists or conspirators, who had tried to assassinate their beloved Führer. It was a nation in denial.

The boot is on the other foot. A captured German soldier is marched off into captivity with the jeers of a hostile crowd ringing in his ears after the liberation of France in 1945. It has been estimated that France lost around 567,000 of its citizens during World War II.

Execution Debate

The Allied leaders realized that something had to be done with the captured Nazi elite – and soon – because the will to pursue those guilty of perpetrating atrocities was swiftly evaporating. Furthermore, the Allied troops were exhausted after five long years of war and they just wanted to go home and put the horrors behind them.

It was well known that the British prime minister, Winston Churchill, favoured the immediate execution of the captured Nazi leaders, in order to avoid the 'tangles of legal procedure', and certain elements within the American administration felt the same. They had managed to persuade President Franklin D. Roosevelt that a cursory hearing followed by a firing squad was the most economical method of dealing with the problem. The British Cabinet had discussed what to do with captured war criminals as far back as June 1942. Anthony Eden, the foreign secretary, had reminded them of the embarrassment caused by their failure to deal decisively with Kaiser Wilhelm II after the First World War.

'The guilt of such individuals is so black,' argued Eden, 'that they fall outside and go beyond the scope of any judicial process.'

Hitler's minions could be dealt with under existing law, but the dictator himself would have to be tried under new laws formulated to deal with the prosecution of a head of state. However, these could be questioned and debated endlessly by the defence. There was a very real danger that Hitler might have turned the proceedings into a show trial, repeating the performance he had given when he was arraigned for treason after the Munich Putsch of 1923. Similar sentiments ran through the American administration. In September 1944, the US secretary of the treasury, Henry Morgenthau Jnr, a close personal friend and adviser to Roosevelt, had even managed to persuade the president and Winston Churchill to sign an agreement to execute captured Nazi leaders. The Nazis had denied their victims a fair trial so why should they deserve a hearing? Besides, there was the very real worry that the accused might use their day in court as a public forum, so they could poison the air with their racist propaganda. And what if the prosecutors failed to secure a conviction? The prospect of an acquittal for any of these 'monsters' was just too hideous to contemplate.

Winston Churchill and Anthony Eden at the Quebec Conference, August 1943.

Lessons of History

Ironically it was the American secretary of war, the elderly Republican Henry
Stimson, who vehemently opposed Morgenthau's plan. He found an unexpected ally
in the Soviet dictator Joseph Stalin, who had told Winston Churchill that if the leading
Nazis were summarily executed the world would say that their enemies had been
afraid to put them on trial and had put them to death to silence them. Stimson added
that to deny the defendants due process would be to risk making them martyrs in the
eyes of their people, which is exactly what had happened after the British had executed
the leaders of the 1916 Easter Rising in Ireland. Stimson recalled that the citizens of
Dublin had initially jeered at the plotters for the destruction they had brought upon
their capital city, but that their mood had altered after the British authorities had
ordered the rebel leaders to be shot without trial.

Stimson had learned the lesson of history and he was determined that America
would not repeat the error. To bolster his argument he brought in a colleague from the
United States War Department, Lieutenant-Colonel Murray Bernays, a former New
York lawyer and an ardent advocate of the principle of justice being seen to be done.
He commissioned Bernays to draw up a practical plan for a public trial and asked him
to establish the legal basis on which the prosecution could assert its authority. Bernays
wrestled with the problem for some considerable time before coming to the conclusion
that Hitler and the Nazi leaders were effectively a criminal regime who had been
engaged in a conspiracy to wage war and enslave the populations of the territories they
conquered. Their intention was to round up and murder the Jews, along with countless
other political enemies and 'undesirables'. The Nazis could therefore be indicted as war
criminals and their atrocities could be categorized as Crimes Against Humanity.

'In Caesar's day the enemy were treated as enemies,' he argued, 'i.e. slaughtered out
of hand if they were not enslaved. In Napoleonic times there was banishment and
imprisonment by what was called political action – now we would impose death –
surely this is retrogression rather than progress.'

On 3 October 1944 Stimson had a meeting with President Roosevelt, during which
he persuaded him that this plan was both practical and morally justifiable.

'The punishment of these men in a dignified manner will have all the greater effect
upon posterity,' he argued.

The Russians were also in favour of the plan and Stimson was confident that the
French and the other formerly occupied nations could be counted on to co-operate if
needed. But there could be no trial without the British. For the next six months the
British government remained stubbornly intractable, insisting that a trial was not
necessary because the accused had already been found guilty in the court of world
opinion. They were not persuaded that execution without trial was contrary to the
British concept of justice.

Following the sudden death of President Roosevelt on 12 April 1945, Vice-President Harry S. Truman took the oath of office. He let it be known that he was frustrated with the lack of progress regarding the trial and was seriously considering establishing an exclusively American tribunal to avoid further delay and dissent. In the event, former Attorney-General Robert Jackson, an associate justice of the United States Supreme Court, would be chief counsel counsel.

American Secretary of War Henry Stimson (left), who was determined to see the Nazi leaders brought to trial, arrives at the White House with Army Chief of Staff George C. Marshall (right) on the day of Franklin D. Roosevelt's funeral, 15 April 1945.

Justice Jackson

'We will show these men to be the living symbols of racial hatred, terrorism and violence, and of the arrogance and cruelty of power.'

CHIEF COUNSEL JUSTICE JACKSON

Jackson was the ideal man for the job. He was committed to the principles of justice and he had a deep-seated distaste for the Nazi regime and the loathsome individuals who had enriched themselves by hanging on to Hitler's coat-tails. In his tailored three-piece suits he cut a commanding figure. He was a dignified presence commanding respect, in contrast to the broken, dishevelled petty bureaucrats and tinpot tyrants he would prosecute.

On 2 May 1945, the day of Jackson's appointment, President Truman asserted his resolve to go to trial with or without the British.

'It is our objective to establish as soon as possible an international military tribunal; and to provide a trial procedure which will be expeditious in nature and which will permit no evasion or delay – but one which is in keeping with our tradition of fairness toward those accused of crime.'

It would be hard for the accused and their fellow countrymen to believe that the Allies were determined to give their enemies a fair hearing, for the Germans had denied their own people justice for 12 years. But Jackson was adamant that the trial would demonstrate the triumph of superior morality rather than superior might, even if it meant that his team was burdened with the 'secular equivalent of redrafting the Ten Commandments'.

When Churchill's War Cabinet met the following day, the British capitulated. They could not afford to be accused of dissent at the forthcoming conference that would mark the founding of the United Nations, nor could they be seen to be denying their defeated enemies a fair trial on the very eve of final victory.

There would be a trial after all.

Robert H. Jackson.

Procedural Procrastination

So much time had been wasted in debating the need for a trial that it came as quite a shock when those charged with its organization realized that there was still no agreement on who would be indicted and on what charges. Four days after the surrender of the German armed forces on 8 May 1945 there were a number of lists in circulation and no consensus as to how the diverse concepts of justice practised by the four Allied powers might be reconciled.

France and the Soviet Union favoured the civil system, whereby accused persons are not permitted to testify but are instead allowed to enter a statement in their own defence at the trial's conclusion. In contrast, the Anglo-American system of common law offers defendants the opportunity to testify under oath, but reserves the closing statement for their legal representatives.

The two systems also differ significantly in terms of procedure, most importantly with regard to the calling of witnesses, who are summoned by the judge within the civil system and by the defence when common law applies. It is possible for dramatic last minute evidence to be introduced by the appearance of a surprise witness during a common law hearing, a possibility that the chief prosecutors at Nuremberg were keen to avoid. Fortunately, a compromise was reached on procedure just before the trial began, which allowed the judges to act as the jury in line with the French system. Even so, the list of those to be indicted remained a matter of heated debate until the eleventh hour.

Although the tribunal was presided over by two judges and a chief counsel from each of the four powers, which made it an international body, the Americans vastly outnumbered their allies. The British team consisted of just 34 members while the Americans supplied more than 200 people, including 25 stenographers, 30 legal experts and six forensic evidence experts. When the British requested more translators, the Cabinet refused. The French offered only a token team. They were content to have a presence at the trial, but they had no desire to pick at the scars inflicted by four years of occupation.

A Difference of Opinion

Jackson's Soviet counterpart was Major-General Iona Nikitchenko, vice-president of the Soviet Supreme Court, who made it known from the outset that he considered it his duty to 'determine the measure of guilt of each particular person and mete out the necessary punishment'. There was no question of acquittal in his mind, a view that was shared by his political masters.

'You must put no man on trial,' Jackson warned, 'if you are not willing to see him freed if not proved guilty. If we want to shoot Germans as a matter of policy, let it be done as such. But don't hide the deed behind a court.'

There were difficulties, too, with the Russian war crimes investigators. They were under orders from Stalin to distance themselves from their Allied counterparts, which undermined the spirit of co-operation needed to convict men who were accused of instigating atrocities committed in various countries. Disagreement and delay dogged the entire process, provoking Jackson into seriously considering resignation. In July, Bernays reported to Washington on the dispiriting progress being made.

'We are deplorably behind schedule on the procurement of the evidence… The trouble is that to do the job we started out to do in the time allowed it looks very much as though we will need a minor miracle, but day by day we are giving the good Lord (and ourselves) less time to work it.'

In the end, sheer dogged determination and persistence on behalf of the American prosecutors finally paid off. The venue for the trial was decided and a date was set.

The Crucible of Fascism

'Nuremberg – once the city of toys, probably the most delightful place in the world for children during the Christmas holidays. With its twelfth-century walls surrounding the old part of the town, its castle on a hilltop, its towers and its spires, its crooked little streets, it looked like something Walt Disney might have created... it now looks as though some angry story-book giant had strode through it... a crumpled tower here, a row of buildings in the dust there.'

YANK MAGAZINE, 8 JUNE 1945

Nuremberg Castle. In addition to the infamous Nazi rallies – at which, in 1935, the anti-Semitic Nuremberg Laws were introduced – another, more ancient event in the town's history made the town an appropriate site for the War Crimes Trials – it had been the site of a pogrom of Jews in 1298.

One of the Nazi rallies held annually in Nuremberg between 1927 and 1938. Nuremberg was chosen as the venue because it had been the unofficial capital of the Holy Roman Empire during its heyday in the medieval and early modern period; Nazi propaganda constantly harkened back to former days of German might and glory.

Nuremberg was, in retrospect, the obvious venue for a public trial of the Nazi war criminals. It had been the site of the massed annual party rallies and it could be seen as the crucible of fascism. What more appropriate place to bring its demigods into the full glare of the public spotlight and reveal them for the 'grotesque and preposterous... clowns and crooks' (according to an Allied report) that they were? The city also offered a sizeable prison containing tiers of single cells, which was largely intact despite the bombing. The Soviets had lobbied for Berlin, but it was not practical because the city was under Soviet occupation. It was also divided into four zones, which would have been a logistical nightmare, and following three years of intense bombing there was not a single prison left standing. In an effort to appease the Russians and to save face the capital was, however, designated as the seat of the tribunal authorities.

At the Potsdam Conference, which began on 16 July 1945, President Truman and the new British prime minister, Clement Attlee – who had defeated Winston Churchill in a landslide election – drafted a communiqué affirming their commitment to a four-power international war crimes tribunal, to be followed by the publication of a list of the defendants. Then on 8 August the Charter of the International Military Tribunal (or London Charter) (see page 28) was signed in London by representatives of the four powers. It set out the character and procedures of the tribunal, with a list of the main charges under the following headings: crimes against peace; war crimes; and crimes against humanity. But even at this late hour the list of defendants was still in dispute.

Charter of the International Military Tribunal (Principal Points)

Article 6

The Tribunal... shall have the power to try and punish persons who, acting in the interests of the European Axis countries, whether as individuals or as members of organizations, committed any of the following crimes.

(a) Crimes against Peace: namely, planning, preparation, initiation or waging of a war of aggression, or a war in violation of international treaties, agreements or assurances, or participation in a Common Plan or Conspiracy for the accomplishment of any of the foregoing;

(b) War Crimes: namely, violations of the laws or customs of war. Such violations shall include, but not be limited to, murder, ill-treatment or deportation to slave labour or for any other purpose of civilian population of or in occupied territory, murder or ill-treatment of prisoners of war or persons on the seas, killing of hostages, plunder of public or private property, wanton destruction of cities, towns, or villages, or devastation not justified by military necessity;

(c) Crimes against Humanity: namely, murder, extermination, enslavement, deportation, and other inhumane acts committed against any civilian population, before or during the war, or persecutions on political, racial, or religious grounds in execution of or in connection with any crime within the jurisdiction of the Tribunal, whether or not in violation of domestic law of the country where perpetrated.

Leaders, organizers, instigators, and accomplices participating in the formulation or execution of a Common Plan or Conspiracy to commit any of the foregoing crimes are responsible for all acts performed by any persons in execution of such plan.

Article 7

The official position of defendants, whether as Heads of State or responsible officials in Government departments, shall not be considered as freeing them from responsibility or mitigating punishment.

Article 16

In order to ensure fair trial for the defendants, the following procedure shall be followed:

(a) The Indictment shall include full particulars specifying in detail the charges against the defendants. A copy of the Indictment and of all the documents lodged with the Indictment, translated into a language which he understands, shall be furnished to the defendant at a reasonable time before the Trial.

(b) During any preliminary examination or trial of a defendant he shall have the right to give any explanation relevant to the charges made against him.

(c) A preliminary examination of a defendant and his trial shall be conducted in, or translated into, a language which the defendant understands.

(d) A defendant shall have the right to conduct his own defence before the Tribunal or to have the assistance of counsel.

(e) A defendant shall have the right through himself or through his counsel to present evidence at the Trial in support of his defence, and to cross-examine any witness called by the Prosecution.

The Question of Conspiracy

The Allied powers had convened a War Crimes Commission as early as September 1943. One of its tasks was to draw up a list of suspected war criminals. Winston Churchill expected the list to include up to one hundred names, some of which would be those of Japanese or Italian participants. However, by the time the date and the venue for the International Tribunal at Nuremberg had been agreed upon the list had been whittled down to those who had served the German state.

The Pacific War was not yet over, so it was agreed that if and when Japan finally surrendered there would be a separate trial to bring those accused of atrocities in the Far East to justice. As for the Italians, their allegiance had shifted with their surrender in 1943, so it was felt that it would not be politically expedient to accuse allies (no matter how recent) of war crimes, particularly in view of the fact that the Italians in the north of the country had been under German occupation since their capitulation.

Despite Clement Attlee's assertion that German officers who had behaved like gangsters should be shot and that German industrialists and financiers who had supported the regime should forfeit their assets, no members of these groups were arraigned when the time came for the final list to be approved. It was felt that it would be impossible to know where to draw the line. Instead one representative from each branch of the regime would stand trial and the prosecution would be charged with revealing their part in a criminal conspiracy to subjugate and enslave the peoples of Europe. It would not be necessary to prove individual acts of barbarity if the defendant was a member of one of the named criminal organizations. The seven named organizations were as follows: the Reich Cabinet; the Leadership Corps of the Nazi Party; the SS; the SA; the Gestapo; the SD; and the General Staff and High Command of the German Armed Forces.

This approach also invalidated the cowardly defence that captured Nazis had offered in mitigation of their crimes – that they had been obeying superior orders. The prisoners were now being tried as participants in a common plan or conspiracy. If convictions were secured against the captured Nazis under these criteria it would make it easier to prosecute their associates and subordinates in future actions, on the grounds that they had shared a collective responsibility. The problem with this strategy was that it would be extremely difficult to prove that the Nazi leadership had planned to dominate Europe from the outset. Hitler had expounded his racist doctrine and his desire for conquest in *Mein Kampf*, but it was implied rather than explicit. The consensus among historians, some of whom acted as advisers to the American prosecution team in 1945, was that Hitler was an opportunist whose aggressive designs took shape as a reaction to events rather than according to a schedule. The Allies were also open to the accusation that they were writing *ex post facto* laws. That is, retroactive laws that make acts criminal that were not criminal when they were committed. In the past, crimes committed in wartime were not considered to be crimes at all.

But the enormity of these offences was undeniable and it was generally accepted that those who endorsed the policy of genocide should answer for the crimes committed in their name, or with their tacit approval. If necessary, new laws would have to be drafted to define these crimes. The traditional legal categories that divided conflicts into either just or unjust wars were grossly inadequate when they were applied to German aggression in the occupied territories. A new law of 'Waging Aggressive War' would have to be drafted, followed by a further law that covered the Nazis' murderous racist policies and the routine terrorization of civilians under occupation. These would be drafted under the heading 'Crimes Against Humanity'. It was a far from ideal situation, but the existing laws governing the breaking of treaties and the flagrant violation of the Geneva Convention and the Hague Convention were woefully inadequate in the face of the Nazis' abominable acts.

The Charges

Count I – Conspiracy: leaders, organizations, instigators, and accomplices in the formulation or execution of a common plan, or conspiracy to commit any of the following crimes are responsible for all acts performed by any persons in execution of such a plan;

Count II – Crimes Against Peace: namely, planning, preparation, initiation or waging of a war of aggression, or a war in violation of international treaties, agreements or assurances, or participation in a common plan or conspiracy for the accomplishment of any of the foregoing;

Count III – War Crimes: namely, violations of the laws or customs of war. Such violations shall include, but not be limited to, murder, ill-treatment or deportation to slave labour or for any other purpose of civilian prisoners of war or persons on the seas, killing of hostages, plunder of public or private property, wanton destruction of cities, towns or villages, or devastation not justified by military necessity;

Count IV – Crimes Against Humanity: namely, murder, extermination, enslavement, deportation, and other inhuman acts committed against any civilian population, before or during the war; or persecutions on political, racial or religious grounds in execution of or in connection with any crime within the jurisdiction of the Tribunal, whether or not in violation of the domestic law of the country where perpetrated.

A Mixed Bag

The pool of prisoners from which the Nazi figureheads were to be taken was severely depleted by the absence of Hitler, Himmler, Goebbels and others who had committed suicide or evaded capture, but there were still enough notorious names to justify the claim, made by the world's press, that the forthcoming proceedings would be the 'trial of the century'.

The Americans had landed Reichsmarschall Hermann Goering, arguably the most prestigious catch. They had also captured a number of individuals who might not have been known to the public but whose deeds would qualify them as some of the most notorious instruments of the Nazi regime. These included Ernst Kaltenbrunner, head of the Reich Main Security Office, who had hoped to evade capture by hiding out in the Austrian Alps under an assumed name. Unfortunately for him, his true identity was unwittingly revealed by his mistress. She was so relieved to see him alive that she did not think to deny that she knew him. Other notable names in American custody included Dr Robert Ley, head of the German Labour Front; Wilhelm Frick, minister of the interior; and Hans Frank, governor-general of Poland. Frank had attempted to evade detection by posing as a German prisoner of war, but his nerves had betrayed him. He slashed his wrists during a suicide attempt and his real identity was revealed during treatment.

Next came the businessmen who had helped Germany prepare for war while making a profit for themselves in the process. The four powers could not come to an agreement about whether they should be represented at Nuremberg or whether they should be detained for a separate trial. The Russians, predictably, were in favour of prosecuting the capitalists who had financed Hitler's war machine and the Americans were inclined to agree, but the British were uncomfortable with the idea of putting the heads of German industry in the dock with mass murderers and high-ranking members of the military. Gustav Krupp, the elderly patriarch of the state's largest steel works, was considered too frail to stand a lengthy trial and some had grave doubts about the inclusion of the former German minister of economics, Hjalmar Schacht, who had engineered Germany's economic recovery in the 1930s. Schacht had initially been an enthusiastic supporter of the regime but he was later incarcerated in Dachau on suspicion of

Arms manufacturer Gustav Krupp (1870–1950) was not tried.

being involved in an attempt to assassinate the Führer on 20 July 1944. This event raised doubts in the minds of the British prosecutors, who were not entirely certain that they were right to arraign him.

No such qualms were voiced over the detention of Julius Streicher, the notorious Jew-baiter and pornographer. His disguise had been penetrated by a Jewish GI, who had casually remarked that he bore a striking resemblance to a wanted war criminal. Streicher misunderstood the GI's poor German and immediately admitted that he was indeed the man the Allies were looking for. The Americans also held Alfred Rosenberg, the self-appointed 'Nazi philosopher' (a contradiction in terms if ever there was one), Franz von Papen (Hitler's vice-chancellor), Walther Funk (successor to Schacht) and Field Marshal Wilhelm Keitel.

The British Batch

The British held Hitler's former deputy Rudolf Hess, whose ill-fated flight to Scotland on 10 May 1941, on what he claimed was a 'peace mission', had led to his capture. It had also raised the question of his mental fitness to stand trial. Also held was Arthur Seyss-Inquart, Reichskommissar of the Netherlands, who held the honorary rank of general in the SS and who was accused of sending an estimated 120,000 of Holland's 140,000 Jews to various death camps. The remainder of the Jews in the Netherlands went into hiding. When the war ended only around 8,000 of them emerged, to be joined by just over 5,000 who had survived the horrors of Mauthausen, Auschwitz, Sobibor and Belsen.

In addition, the British also boasted a handful of high-profile defendants such as General Alfred Jodl, chief of operations, Albert Speer, Hitler's architect and armaments minister and Admiral Doenitz, Hitler's nominal successor. Following the Führer's suicide, Doenitz set up a new 'government' with the sole purpose of gaining the authority to surrender. His capture was, however, scant compensation for the conspicuous absence of SS Reichsführer Heinrich Himmler, who had surrendered to the British in May only to commit suicide by biting into a cyanide capsule that had been hidden in his teeth.

But in June 1945 the British were able to add Joachim von Ribbentrop to their trophies, after receiving a tip-off informing them that the former Nazi foreign minister was hiding in an apartment in Hamburg. He went meekly into captivity dressed in pink-striped pyjamas and clutching a washbag containing his toiletries, 100,000 marks and a personal letter to 'Vincent' Churchill, in which he spoke of Hitler as a 'great idealist'. The money, he confessed, was to keep him clothed and fed until such time as the danger of the death penalty had passed and public opinion had moderated to the point when he could re-emerge, to be venerated as a politician and not a criminal.

A Show of Unity

For their part the French were guarding Baron Konstantin von Neurath, former German foreign minister and Reichsprotektor of Bohemia. The Soviet Union contributed only two names to the list of accused – Goebbels' deputy Hans Fritzsche and Grand Admiral Erich Raeder – but they had 20 million ghosts behind them demanding justice, so no one questioned their commitment to the trial.

Nevertheless, when the Soviets protested against the principle of a trial for Nazi butchers such as Gestapo chief Ernst Kaltenbrunner, Jackson was forced to remind them that they were free to conduct a separate hearing with the two men they held, if they wished.

It was a cheap shot, but Jackson knew that the integrity of the tribunal depended on the public unity of the four powers, who must be seen to set aside their differences for the common good.

Although the prosecutors had gone to great pains to ensure that the accused would be given a fair trial, they were acutely aware that they would be doing so in the full glare of the world's press. They also realized that there was a very real danger that both the press and the public might lose interest if the proceedings were allowed to become bogged down in points of procedure, or if the 'wrong' defendants were in the dock. The Rule of Law would be enforced whether there was an audience to witness it in action or not, and anyone who had served the dictatorship would qualify for a seat in the dock whether they were dull, duped or demented, but the proceedings would have no impact if the world turned its back.

People were weary of war and wanted to put it all behind them, but the fact is that they could not afford to forget and should not be allowed to do so. The trial needed personalities or it was in danger of becoming a footnote in the history books.

Propagandist Hans Fritzsche (left) and Grand Admiral Raeder were both taken prisoner by the Red Army at the time of the fall of Berlin.

CHAPTER TWO

THE ACCUSED

Goering once boasted that some day there would be statues of him erected in every town and city in Germany. If the Nuremberg Trials had not taken place his prediction might have been fulfilled, even though his inflated sense of self-importance had led to him being portrayed as a comic figure during the war. Newspaper cartoonists made fun of his enormous girth and his fondness for uniforms and medals, which were more in keeping with a character in a comic operetta. But there was nothing amusing about the real Hermann Goering. He was a vain, vindictive, arrogant and uncommonly cruel individual, whose thin veneer of charm rapidly disintegrated when he was faced with anyone who dared to disagree with him.

He once confessed that the only man who intimidated him was Hitler. Everyone else needed to watch their step or they would find their name noted in his notorious black book. One thing that could be said in his favour was that he had the patience of a snake. He could wait years, if necessary, to settle a score. It was his arrogance and his need to strut once more upon the world stage that prevented him from taking his own life in the latter days of the Third Reich. But he might also have wanted to ensure the safety of his wife and children by delivering them personally into the hands of the Americans. Having done so he would then have had the opportunity to demonstrate what a convivial guest he could be.

In the absence of Hitler he was the face of the Third Reich. His presence at the trial would ensure that the reporters took their seats every day and that they would be there to witness the unmasking of the man who was responsible for the establishment of the Gestapo and the network of concentration camps. After the trial no one found Reichsmarschall Goering amusing any more.

The Uninvited Guest

On the evening of 7 May 1945, a convoy of German vehicles pushed through the surging columns of refugees on the Austrian road that wound towards the American lines, like a ship ploughing against the tide. A jumble of suitcases had been strapped to the dark saloon at the head of the line. As it emerged from the sea of people and turned off the road towards Fischhorn Castle, near Zell am See, the two young sentries noticed that Nazi pennants fluttered from the front wheel rims. They raised their rifles and aimed at the driver who slowed down and then turned the engine off. A moment later the rear door swung open and to the astonishment of the sentries a little girl with blond ringlets and a pretty party dress emerged. She was clutching a large doll. Right behind her was a stout middle-aged woman in a flower-patterned skirt and blouse, complete with a black fur stole, a pearl necklace and a pink hat fringed with a small lace veil. They looked as if they were dressed for church. Their sudden appearance brought other GIs to the wire to stare. Then the driver's door swung wide and a familiar figure emerged. The man was dressed in full military uniform, with an Iron Cross pinned to his breast and another at his throat, just above the gold clasp that

Ever a lover of the limelight, Hermann Goering sits and talks with US soldiers and members of the press.

secured his cape. There was no mistaking the figure of Reichsmarschall Hermann Goering. At that moment he raised his hands in surrender. Pulling in behind him were 17 truck-loads of personal possessions. Goering evidently expected to be treated like a political prisoner – a respected, vanquished foe.

The commanding officer, General Stack, was immediately summoned. He cursed under his breath when he caught sight of the former chief of the Luftwaffe. Goering introduced his wife and child. The American nodded politely, still unable to take in the full gravity of the situation. Goering broke the silence by drawing his ceremonial dagger from its sheath and presenting it handle first, in a formal gesture of surrender. He then extended a pudgy hand, which was taken enthusiastically. The tension was broken, there were smiles all round and the unit photographer was sent for to capture the moment for posterity.

The war was over, the monster Hitler was dead and many of his henchmen were in captivity. There was cause for celebration. It seemed peevish not to invite their most prominent prisoner to the party. That afternoon and late into the night the officer's mess rang with endless rounds of American popular songs and toasts to the war's end. Before the festivities wrapped up, Goering was persuaded to perform his own party piece. He obliged by singing a round of sentimental German drinking songs while accompanying himself on the accordion. More photographs were taken.

The next morning these appeared in newspapers around the world, to the dismay of the Allied prosecution team, who feared that this instance of fraternization would undermine their case against the defendants. If their own armed forces were prepared to forgive and forget so easily, what hope was there of re-educating the German people?

'War is like a football game. Whoever loses gives his opponent his hand, and everything is forgotten.'

HERMANN GOERING

The Skeletal City

The picturesque medieval city where once the Meistersingers had celebrated German culture, and where the artist Dürer had been born, had been all but obliterated by no fewer than 11 major bombing raids. A quarter of a million of Nuremberg's inhabitants had been left homeless and 6,000 bodies were said to lie unburied under mounds of rubble. The stench of decomposition was partially masked by the equally pungent fumes of gallons and gallons of disinfectant, the water supply was contaminated, there was no electricity or gas and the sewage system was not functioning.

The front of the Grand Hotel in Nuremberg during repairs. It was the only building left standing that was capable of housing the Allied prosecution teams. Although about 90 per cent of the medieval heart of the town was destroyed by Allied bombing, much was rebuilt after the war, including the reconstruction of some of its medieval buildings.

The Marble Room inside the Grand Hotel, Nuremberg, where a special evening of traditional German folk culture is laid on for members of the International Military Tribunal (IMT).

In the summer of 1945 the only building with electric light and hot running water was the Grand Hotel, which American engineers had renovated to provide 270 rooms, a night club and a gymnasium for the Allied prosecution teams. In the evenings cheap music would drift across the wasteland of the shattered city from the dance floor. It was the only sign of life in the ruins.

But the survivors did not feel that they were at all to blame for what had taken place in the war years. When Jackson went to check on how the renovation of the Palace of Justice was coming along, in preparation for the trial, he was confronted by groups of shabbily dressed women. They were on their way to scavenge what they could from the few shops that were still standing. Their clothes were as colourless as their gaunt, sour faces and their only expression was one of hatred for the soldiers, who stared back as if they were looking at a lost tribe. The troops were no doubt mindful of the army information films, which reminded them that these same civilians were the ones who had cheered Hitler through the streets only a few years earlier, their arms raised in the Führer salute, their eyes glazed as they looked on their Messiah and their throats hoarse from crying, 'Sieg Heil'. They were not sorry for supporting the war, only for having lost it. The trial would force them to listen to those who had suffered far worse than the loss of their homes.

An armoured car guards the approach to the Palace of Justice in the background. The courtroom is on the second floor and can be identified by the white windows.

The Palace of Justice

The shell-scarred Palace of Justice resembled a besieged fortress in bandit country. It had been the site of the final battle for the city. The courtyard was still strewn with pieces of shrapnel and spent cartridges where the remnants of two SS divisions had held out until they had been shelled into submission. Now five Sherman tanks squatted at key points around the main building, their gun barrels loaded with 76 mm shells, while GIs crouched behind sandbags at the entrance to the court.

More troops were on guard on the ground floor. They stood stiffly to attention, looking as rigid as the marble pillars, while other GIs stood outside the administration offices on the floor above. In the cell block to the rear of the courthouse the sentries were armed with automatic weapons. No one was taking any chances. There were rumours that fanatical bands of SS 'Werewolves' – led by the elusive Martin Bormann, Hitler's sycophantic secretary – might stage a suicide raid to free the prisoners. Ludicrous though it might sound in retrospect, the prospect of a final blood sacrifice in the city that had been a bastion of National Socialism was very real in the minds of those charged with guarding the last of the Hitler gang. Even in the shattered city, a few fanatics were still fighting a lost war by stringing steel wire across the streets to decapitate the drivers of American jeeps, which had been fitted with vertical steel bars to cut through any such obstructions.

The trial date had been set for 20 November, which was less than eight weeks away. It was a tight schedule. Fortunately the Palace of Justice had remained structurally sound despite the heavy bombing, but the building was clearly in need of extensive repairs. The main courtroom was chaotic. Chairs lay overturned on the floor, cases of Coca-Cola and petrol cans were piled on desks and the dark wooden panelling was pockmarked, not with woodworm but with bullet holes. Building materials were as rare as veal cutlets in the city, so they had to be brought in from elsewhere. Labour, however, was in plentiful supply. SS prisoners of war were ordered to clean up the mess so the craftsmen could move in and begin the renovation.

An initial inspection had revealed that the principal court room was far too small for such a momentous trial, so it would have to be enlarged. This would mean demolishing a wall to accommodate the larger than usual dock, while a raised dais would have to be built for the eight judges. In addition, dozens of legal representatives would need to be housed and there would have to be a glass booth for the interpreters, a press gallery and seating for up to 500 spectators. The only original features to be retained were the chandeliers, three bronze plaques that were affixed to marble pillars in the entrance hall and the coat of arms behind the judge's bench. This last item was inscribed with the Ten Commandments, an ironic feature considering that Nuremberg had given its name to the infamous laws that had deprived the German Jews of their rights.

The three bronze plaques depicted Adam and Eve in the Garden of Eden, symbolizing temptation. This scene was flanked by the figure of Justice, with an unsheathed sword, and a depiction of the Roman fasces, a spray of rods and axes that symbolized the authority of the state. In the final phase of reconstruction the courtroom was fitted with a sound system that promised simultaneously translated testimony in three languages. All of the participants could select the language of their choice at the flick of a switch, which would then be fed into their headphones. The same service was available to the press and the public. In case anyone spoke too fast for the interpreters, warning lights were installed in the witness box.

The work of reconstruction progressed steadily, the young GI in charge of the project improvising where necessary. He commandeered seating from a nearby theatre and whatever else he needed that could not be built on site.

The reconstruction of the old courtroom, which involved the removal of one wall and incorporation of the adjoining room.

Serving the Indictments

When former artillery officer Airey Neave returned to Germany in August 1945, as a member of the British War Crimes Executive, he did so with no desire for revenge and no hatred for the ordinary German soldier. He had savoured a personal victory over the Germans several years earlier, when he had crossed the border into Switzerland after having escaped from the formidable prisoner of war camp at Colditz Castle and he considered that he had been fairly treated by his captors. The only exception was a grilling by the Gestapo during an earlier escape attempt. He was just 29 years old, but his experiences had aged him considerably.

Having been educated in Berlin in the early 1930s, he spoke German fluently and his subsequent experiences as an intelligence agent for M19 gave him a unique insight into the Nazi mentality. His superiors intended to capitalize on these skills by getting him to accumulate evidence against the armaments manufacturer Gustav Krupp and the industrial dynasty he headed. The Americans described the members of the dynasty as 'the most vicious instruments of Teutonic aggression'. In the event, Gustav did not stand trial due to failing health, but Neave gathered sufficient evidence to have his son Alfried convicted in a subsequent trial. When the decision was made to abandon the case against the ailing Gustav Krupp, Neave was seconded to the tribunal as a judicial aide. He was given the honour of serving the indictments on each of the defendants in their cells at Nuremberg, although the privilege was purely political. The Americans knew that they could not be seen to be running the whole show. It was typical of the haste, and the improvisational nature, of the proceedings that Neave was not given time to read the weighty documents that were still being copied the night before he was due to serve them.

The cells in Nuremberg jail occupied by the main defendants. Each prisoner was constantly watched by a guard at his door.

Face to Face

On the afternoon of Friday 19 October Major Neave entered the prison block at the rear of the courthouse, accompanied by Colonel Andrus the prison warden,

Harold B. Willey, chief clerk to the United States Supreme Court, and an interpreter. As the massive iron doors swung open, the bright autumn sun broke through a high window at the far end of the building. This illuminated the cavernous interior enough to give the party a glimpse of the three tiers of cells laced with wire netting and the spiral staircase at the rear. The main defendants were held in solitary cells on the ground floor, lesser war criminals were kept on the second tier and the top floor was reserved for the female concentration camp guards. Only 20 out of the original 24 defendants were present on the day of the indictments. Admiral Raeder and Hans Fritzsche, Goebbels' deputy, were still being held in the Russian zone – they were not transferred to Nuremberg until the end of October – Gustav Krupp was too ill to be tried and Martin Bormann was missing. He was later sentenced to death *in absentia*.

Colonel B. C. Andrus, referred to by some of the prisoners as 'the fireman' because of his badge and helmet.

A master sergeant who held the keys to each of the cells on a large ring thrust a pen at Neave. He ordered him to sign and he noted the time. The fierce and formidable Colonel Andrus had drilled into his detachment the need to do everything by the book. He had also made it plain that they were to treat their charges as criminals and not as prisoners of war. There was to be no saluting or fraternization. His men had seen their friends killed as they had fought their way across Germany and they had witnessed the carnage and destruction for which these men were responsible. Behind his steel-rimmed spectacles, Andrus rarely smiled. He had reputedly told Goering that he would put him on a diet to ensure that he was fit and healthy to be hanged.

The party was joined by the prison chaplain, a lieutenant-colonel from the American security staff, Dr Kelley, the prison psychiatrist, and a number of white-helmeted military policemen. All of them walked in silence until they came to a cell near the end of the row.

'Goering,' said Colonel Andrus, betraying no emotion.

Goering – Godfather of Terrorism

'[Goering was] one of the cruellest political criminals of all time... the Godfather of terrorism.'

MAJOR AIREY NEAVE

Neave peered through the small iron grill and caught a glimpse of the 53-year-old former Reichsmarschall sitting on his bunk. His face was frozen in a grimace, as if he had woken from a bad dream only to find that he had not been asleep at all. Entering the 13 by 9 foot cell, Neave's anxiety drained away. Goering was a short squat caricature of his former blustering self, his mind and body ravaged by an addiction to morphine. During his initial interrogation, one of his 16 monogrammed suitcases had been found to contain 20,000 paracodeine pills, a prescription painkiller.

Neave did not find Goering intimidating, merely pitiful – there was something 'indefinably feminine' about him. Although he was not a homosexual he had greeted his captors at Fischhorn Castle with red-painted fingernails. The spartan prison diet had

Goering eating a meal in his cell. Stripped of his flamboyant uniform and medals – and boasting a much smaller girth due to prison rations – he cut a far less intimidating figure than in former days.

reduced his weight from 20
stones to 15 stones in just six
weeks so his uniform, stripped of
all medals and insignia, now
hung loosely around his bulky
frame. He reminded Neave of a
dissolute Roman emperor, the
more so because it was known
that he had attended official
parties in a toga and sandals, with
rouged cheeks and wearing a
large amount of jewellery. Now
all of that gaudy opulence was
gone and his empire was in ruins.

*Goering's few remaining personal possessions photographed in
his cell while he was attending a session of the trial.*

The tiny cell was
claustrophobic, an odour of
staleness and decay pervaded the
air. A small barred window shed enough light to reveal that the steel bed was fastened
to the floor and dabs of fresh plaster betrayed the fact that metal hooks had been dug
out of the wall, for fear that the prisoners might be tempted to cut their wrists.
There was a toilet and a wash bowl with running water, as well as a table upon which
Goering had arranged a framed family photograph and a small pile of books. The only
other item of furniture was a chair, which was removed at night in case anyone wanted
to follow the example of Dr Conti, one of Hitler's medical advisers, who had hanged
himself in his cell on 6 October. Conti had been accused of conducting hideous
experiments on human beings.

Neave contrasted the comparative luxury of the cell with the conditions in which
he had been incarcerated in Poland. Even worse than that were the appalling
conditions endured by dozens of child slave workers at the Krupp steel works at Essen.
He remembered, too, the prisoner who had attempted to keep a photograph of his
parents, only to be brutally beaten for the offence by the Krupp guards. They ripped
the picture up in front of him, out of sheer spite. Neave overcame his initial fear of
this once formidable figure and returned his gaze – Goering's 'small and greedy' eyes
looked away.

When Neave introduced himself, Goering rose to his feet to face him. He bowed
stiffly and smiled, a hint of geniality in his eyes, and then gestured towards the bed
as if to say, 'I'm sorry but I cannot offer you a seat'. However, his expression
changed to a scowl when he was handed the indictment and Neave informed him
of his right to conduct his own defence or obtain the assistance of counsel. Dr
Kelley recorded his response.

'So it has come,' Goering said gloomily. He took the documents without looking
at them.

Hess – An Act of Madness

'None knew better than Hess how determined Hitler was to realize his ambitions and by what methods.'

JUDGMENT OF THE NUREMBERG TRIBUNAL 1946

Neave's attitude towards Rudolf Hess, the former deputy Führer captured by the British in May 1941, was ambivalent. He was aware that many believed that the bushy-browed hypochondriac who had once served as Hitler's secretary was insane but harmless. They had argued that his enforced absence disqualified him as a war criminal. But there was no denying that Hess had been an integral part of the regime prior to the outbreak of war. He had been a signatory to the Nuremberg Laws, which had been the first step towards the genocide of the Jews, he had been a vociferous supporter of rearmament and he had oiled the wheels of the Nazi war machine by using his obsequious charm to bring the likes of Krupp and Hitler together.

When they left Hess's cell, Colonel Andrus confided his doubts to Major Neave.

'We've only had this guy Hess a week. We think he is shamming, but we are taking no chances. He tried to commit suicide over in England.'

In fact, Hess had made two attempts. He had leapt from a height in 1942, fracturing his thigh, and three years later he had stabbed himself in the chest with a bread knife. His paranoia had led him to accuse his captors of trying to poison him, but the prison doctors at Nuremberg had judged him legally sane and fit to stand trial.

When the cell door was unlocked, Neave was asked to wait while a white-helmeted military policeman went ahead and handcuffed the prisoner. As Neave watched through the tiny window he caught his first sight of the cadaverous, shrunken figure whose thick, dark eyebrows contrasted so garishly with his pallid skin. When Major Neave entered, Hess stood to attention and grinned inanely but said nothing. He was dressed in a grey tweed coat and flying boots, his thin manacled hand raised in a gesture of contempt. His wild appearance was disturbing. Neave handed him the three documents he had been instructed to serve – the indictment, a copy of the charter on which the tribunal had been founded and a list of German lawyers. Hess listened as his rights were read and then he asked if he could defend himself. It was not the reaction of a lunatic. He was clearly lucid but if he were given the opportunity to speak in his own defence he might make a mockery of the court. Suddenly he became convulsed with stomach cramps – a symptom of his hypochondria – and was allowed to sit on the bed until the attack subsided. After he had recovered he rose unsteadily to his feet and asked meekly if he was going to be tried with Goering and the other party 'comrades'. When he was told that he was being charged with taking part in a conspiracy with the other Nazi leaders and that they would therefore be put on trial together, he replied that he would not like to be tried with Goering.

Speaking of the murderous nature of the regime and of Hitler, Hess remarked, 'It is just incomprehensible how those things came about... Every genius has the demon in him. You can't blame him – it is just in him... It is all very tragic.'

Then he returned to his paperback. The indictment lay on the bed, but he was evidently not inclined to look at it.

Von Ribbentrop – Hitler's Champagne Salesman

'We are only living shadows – the remains of a dead era – an era that died with Hitler. Whether a few of us live another 10 or 20 years, it makes no difference.'

JOACHIM VON RIBBENTROP, 27 MARCH 1946

The next cell was occupied by Joachim von Ribbentrop, the former champagne salesman who became Nazi foreign minister in 1938 and was responsible for negotiating the Nazi-Soviet Non-Aggression Pact in 1939. This freed Hitler to invade Europe without fear of Soviet intervention. Hitler had dubbed von Ribbentrop 'the second Bismarck', in reference to the distinguished German statesman who united the former Prussian states into one nation, but professional diplomats despised him. They considered him contemptible and tactless. When presenting his credentials to King Edward VIII at Buckingham Palace, he had given the Hitler salute, an unforgivable insult. Even the Axis allies regarded him with derision. Mussolini famously remarked that Ribbentrop was 'truly sinister because he is an imbecile and truly presumptuous'. His fellow defendants shared that view. Schacht remarked that von Ribbentrop should be hanged for his stupidity if nothing else and prison psychiatrist Dr G.M. Gilbert saw him as 'a confused and demoralized opportunist'.

Ribbentrop certainly cut a pathetic figure as he stood there in his carpet slippers, shaking from head to foot in his shabby civilian suit. He wrung his hands and avoided the gaze of his jailers as Neave, Andrus and the interpreter entered. Looking much older than his 52 years, his grey hair was thinning, there was a pained expression on his gaunt face and his eyes were moist with tears. He shifted uneasily as the indictment was read out. When he spoke it was in a shrill, piping voice that seemed at odds with his former official status. But

Joachim von Ribbentrop writing a letter while in custody awaiting trial.

now he was merely a prisoner, whose furtive glances suggested that he was frantically searching for a way out. Goering had described him as a 'boundless egotist', but now he was consumed by self-pity.

'What am I to do?' he asked. 'Where am I to find a lawyer?'

He handed Neave a handwritten list containing the names of members of the British aristocracy. 'They can give evidence of my desire for peace.'

His self-delusion amused the major, who recalled that von Ribbentrop had once told Hitler that Britain was decadent and lacked fighting spirit.

'You will help me please, Herr Major?' he pleaded, his voice cracking with emotion.

Streicher – The Beast of Nuremberg

'For twenty-five years he educated the German people in the philosophy of hate, of brutality, of murder. He incited and prepared them to support the Nazi policy, to accept and participate in the brutal persecution and slaughter of his fellow men. Without him these things could not have been. It is long since he forfeited all right to live.'

THE BRITISH PROSECUTION, NUREMBERG 1946

Julius Streicher was the only defendant who had been incarcerated at Nuremberg on a previous occasion, when he had been jailed on charges of indecency. During an official visit to the cells as *Gauleiter* of Franconia he had assaulted a young boy with a bull whip and gloated that it had given him an orgasm.

The bullet-headed 'Beast of Nuremberg' was essentially a sex criminal whose unhealthy obsession with his own gratification led him to boast of nightly wet dreams – and he would produce the semen to prove it. He was in the habit of asking children if they masturbated and he was proud of his vast collection of pornography, one of the largest in Germany. But he was not only a degenerate. He was also a sadist and a rabid anti-Semite.

The day after *Kristallnacht*, when Nazi sympathizers smashed Jewish shops and burnt synagogues to the ground, goaded by the brown-shirted stormtroopers of the SA, Streicher made a telling declaration.

Defiant to the very end, the archetypal bully Julius Streicher in his cell.

'We know there are still people who pity the Jew. They are not worthy of living in this city, nor are they worthy of belonging to this nation... In bygone days Nuremberg citizens burned down the synagogue which was no house of God but a murderer's den. Today we admire those men and say they lived in a great epoch. In centuries to come people will say the same of our time.'

From 1933 to 1940 Streicher wielded almost limitless power as a *Gauleiter*. He also published *Der Stürmer*, a virulently pornographic publication in which he accused Jews of taking part in ritualistic bloodletting ceremonies to appease their God. His journal also claimed that they preyed on innocent Aryan girls.

Educated Nazis despised him and even his fellow defendants protested that they found it offensive to be tried with this 'obscene dwarf'. But although he was stripped of his official powers in 1940 for 'corruption' – that is, stealing property owned by Jews before Goering could do so – no one in the Nazi hierarchy denounced his pornographic propaganda. That was because they shared his beliefs and sniggered at his crude, offensive jokes.

One of the most insidious crimes of the Hitler regime was its endorsement of *Der Stürmer*, which was read aloud to schoolchildren. In 1936 a letter from a girl pupil was printed in the publication. She described how her class, inspired by its articles, had staged plays about Jews and she went on to say that they had made a doll with 'a nose like Satan', to represent a Jew. But this was not enough to satisfy Streicher, who decided to publish a series of repulsive anti-Semitic books for children – two of which were *The Jewish Question in the Classroom* and *The Poisonous Fungus*, both illustrated by his young readers. By these means Streicher infected an entire generation with the poison of anti-Semitism.

Major Neave spoke of him with revulsion, describing Streicher as 'stupid, cunning and cruel'. He was 60 years old at the time of the trial, stocky but strong as a bull. When he was not pacing his cell 'like an ape exposing himself in a cage', he stood with his hands on his hips in a gesture of defiance, the archetypal bully. His khaki shirt had been left open to expose his hairy chest. Neave reflected that in former times Streicher would have made an enthusiastic interrogator for the Inquisition.

As Neave entered the cell to read the indictment, Streicher was puffing and blowing like a cornered gorilla. He opened his mouth and hissed, which made Colonel Andrus order him to be quiet. After the indictment was read to him he demanded that he be given the name of an anti-Semitic lawyer.

'A Jew could not defend me,' he ranted in a shrill voice.

He followed this surreal moment with another, when he accused the judges of being prejudiced because they too were Jews. Then he gave Neave a lewd wink and said, 'The Herr Major is not a Jew'.

Andrus cut him short, but before the party left the cell Streicher asked for the services of Dr Marx, a lawyer. 'I am without friends,' he added. Neave noted this statement without surprise or sympathy.

Von Schirach – The Self-Centred Socialite

'About 1942, I think I first began to notice that Hitler was becoming slightly insane...'

BALDUR VON SCHIRACH

Baldur von Schirach, the 38-year-old former Nazi Youth Leader and *Gauleiter* of Vienna, was an entirely different species. A vain, aristocratic intellectual he had written florid poetry in praise of Hitler and was said to boast of having a white boudoir with lace curtains, like a latter-day Madame de Pompadour. He looked faintly ridiculous when he was photographed in uniform or Bavarian shorts, like an overgrown schoolboy in fancy dress. It was characteristic of him that he had dismissed the death of millions as a 'misfortune' – the result of 'racial politics'. The war had been an unsavoury interruption in his life of socializing and self-indulgence.

In spite of being deprived of his liberty and his luxuries, Schirach would not allow his appearance or his standards to suffer. When Major Neave and his party arrived he was dressed in a neatly pressed dove-grey suit, as if he were greeting his guests at a tea dance. But there was something repellent and unpleasant about him. It might have been his affectations and his mannered speech, or his suspect sexuality, that gave Neave the impression that he was the type of man 'who would be a danger to small boys'. Of more immediate concern were the serious questions concerning Schirach's part in the transportation of Austrian Jews from Vienna to extermination camps in Poland and his intimate knowledge of the activities of the *Einsatzgruppen*, to which he was privy as Reich Defence Commissioner.

He treated his 'guests' to an ingratiating smile when they arrived and he greeted the reading of the indictment with faintly feminine reproof, like a school teacher leafing through a badly written essay. Given the opportunity, von Schirach looked as if he might respond with a critique of its style and content rather than a plea of 'Not Guilty'.

'I must think this over,' he said condescendingly.

The coldly dispassionate and creepily fastidious von Schirach spent much of his time in his cell reading.

Rosenberg – The Foolish Philosopher

'He had the greatest capacity for making the simplest proposition complicated and obscure.'

MAJOR AIREY NEAVE

When Neave's party stepped into the next cell, the contrast could not have been more marked. Alfred Rosenberg had revelled in his self-appointed title of 'Nazi philosopher', but it was a blatant misnomer if ever there was one – he had been a second-rate mind in a corrupt collective of criminals, sadists, sexual perverts and petty bureaucrats. Now there was nothing left but a dejected, pathetic figure brushing breadcrumbs from his crumpled suit. He wore a dour expression which Neave described as being a cross between an off-duty undertaker and a 'sick spaniel' and he was trembling from head to foot as the party approached.

Rosenberg was an Estonian by birth, whose dark complexion looked out of place when he was penned in with his fellow defendants in the dock. It was no secret that he had a Jewish mistress, which prompted some to speculate that he might be 'the only Aryan Rosenberg in the world'.

Rosenberg was portrayed as one of the key architects of Nazi racial theory.

Hitler had held Rosenberg in such obvious contempt that it was still a mystery why he had appointed him to positions with pretentious titles but no power. It can only have been done as a perverse private joke. Perhaps he enjoyed watching him squirm at every insult, like a jester who had been hired to keep the court amused. Goering also despised Rosenberg and Goebbels dismissed his book, *The Myth of the Twentieth Century*, as an 'ideological belch'. Hitler told Rosenberg to his face that it was 'an intelligent book', but in private he sneered that it was 'illogical rubbish'.

However, this facade of shabby incompetence belied Rosenberg's true nature. As Reich Minister for the Occupied Eastern Territories he supervised the theft of art treasures across Europe. In Paris alone 38,000 properties were looted as part of what Rosenberg boasted was the 'biggest art operation in history'. His defence was that the Allies had robbed Germany of property worth 25 billion marks after the First World War – but as the judges were to remark, one alleged crime does not justify the commitment of another.

Self-deluded to the last, Rosenberg rejected the indictment.

'The anti-Semitic movement was only protective,' he said. 'Just as I wanted *Lebensraum* for Germany, I thought Jews should have a *Lebensraum* for themselves – outside Germany.'

It was ironic that his considered response to the charges was to ask if he could be legally represented by the prisoner in the adjoining cell – Dr Hans Frank, 'the Butcher of Poland'.

Frank – The Butcher of Poland

'We must not be squeamish when we hear the figure of 17,000 shot.'

HANS FRANK

During his first escape from the Gestapo, Major Neave had been sheltered by several Polish families. They had told him of the cruelty inflicted on their countrymen because of the orders of the man he now stood face to face with in the squalid cell at Nuremberg.

Hans Frank struck Neave as 'half-mad'. His eyes rolled, he perspired profusely and he muttered a half-coherent response when he was handed the documents detailing the charges.

At first he had blamed Hitler and his fellow accused for his downfall and present ignominious plight. Then he took refuge in religion. He reaffirmed his faith in the Catholic Church and in God, whom he thanked for bringing him before the 'world court' so that he might redeem himself and seek forgiveness. It was a performance that convinced some, but it reminded Neave of Dr Pritchard, the Victorian murderer, who kissed the corpse of the wife he had poisoned and then sought absolution in his Bible. Frank's sham contrition filled Neave with revulsion.

While Europe starved, Frank had lived the high life, dining on delicacies smuggled across the border from Germany. Even the SS had him under surveillance for hoarding furs and jewellery bought under duress from frightened Jews at a fraction of their true value, valuables that he neglected to declare to his Nazi bosses. When Hitler heard about Frank's audacious activities he laughed, knowing that he could have him arrested at a moment's notice and his booty transported to Berlin. But it suited his purpose to keep Frank in power until he had outlived his usefulness. He was simply too efficient to replace.

But the former lawyer was no fool. Like any self-respecting shyster he had insured himself by keeping detailed diaries, which he handed over to the Americans on the day of his capture. They were incriminating in the extreme. One entry read, 'We must annihilate the Jews wherever we find them and wherever possible.' Another declared that, 'I have not been hesitant in declaring that when a German is shot, up to 100 Poles shall be shot too.'

Their author's protestations that he was two people – the weak private personality and the Nazi 'louse', each acting independently of the other – struck the prison psychologists as a pathetic attempt to absolve himself of responsibility for his deplorable actions.

Despite his profuse declarations of guilt, even Frank's own son disowned him, doubting the sincerity of his hand-wringing remorse.

A career confidence trickster, Hans Frank's protestations of remorse and his desire to atone for his crimes through his death deceived few people at the International Military Tribunal in Nuremberg.

'Don't let anybody tell you that they had no idea. Everybody sensed there was something horribly wrong with the system.'

HANS FRANK, 29 NOVEMBER 1945

Funk – Hitler's Chief Cashier

**'I signed the laws for the Aryanization of Jewish property.
Whether that makes me legally guilty or not, is another matter.
But it makes me morally guilty, there is no doubt about that.'**

WALTHER FUNK

*Walther Funk seemed a feeble figure when Major
Neave presented him with his indictment.*

Walther Funk made no attempt to hide his emotions. When Neave entered the cell of the 55-year-old former president of the Reichsbank, he found him sitting on his bed weeping uncontrollably. He rose when ordered by Colonel Andrus and then stood shaking in a long tweed coat that had been given to him as a concession to his ill health. His face was flaccid, betraying the ravages of alcoholism, but then many Nazi officials had drunk themselves to excess. It was the only way they could live with themselves.

'Be a man, Funk,' barked the colonel. 'Listen to the major.'

When Funk had been taken into custody at the Allied detention centre at Mondorf-les-Bains he had confessed to Colonel Andrus that he had personally ordered the murder of Jews so that he could have their gold teeth removed and deposited in his vaults. He had also requested that gold teeth be removed from slave workers and their spectacles collected for export to Germany. In another admission he said that he had discovered that the robes of rabbis were embroidered with precious metals, so he had them confiscated and picked clean of their golden thread. When he stood in the witness box at Nuremberg he would deny having made that confession, even when he was confronted with SS witness Oswald Pohl, who had accompanied him on a boastful tour of his vaults.

He took the indictment and dried his eyes.

'I must see my counsel at once,' he said, pulling himself together. 'I have a great interest in the outcome of this trial.'

'So has the whole world,' Neave replied.

Frick – Servant of the State

'Hitler didn't want to do things my way. I wanted things done legally. After all, I am a lawyer.'

WILHELM FRICK, 24 APRIL 1946

Wilhelm Frick did not put on an act of remorse or take refuge in self-pity and denial. Instead he stood erect and defiant, his fierce eyes flashing and his closely-cropped hair bristling like a Prussian officer of the old school. Even in his fawn tweed jacket, the

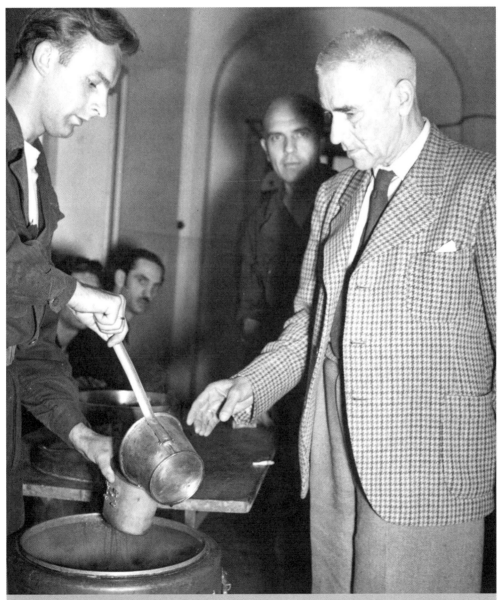

Wilhelm Frick is served his supper ration in Nuremberg jail. Unlike some of his fellow defendants, he maintained his standards of personal grooming during incarceration.

elderly former minister of the interior still cut a formidable figure. It was easy to imagine him condemning to death the thousands of physically and mentally handicapped victims he had branded as dispensable. He would have issued decrees for the implementation of the Nazi New Order with the same bureaucratic indifference.

A tiresome pedant, he was tactless to an extreme. Speaking in his bleating, high-pitched voice, he once told Hitler that his father's beatings had done him no end of good. It was no surprise that he responded with incredulity to the charges detailed in the indictment. What could he – a mere functionary of the administration – have possibly known of its criminal conspiracy to wage aggressive war and enslave millions?

Kaltenbrunner – Himmler's Stooge

'When I saw the newspaper headline "GAS CHAMBER EXPERT CAPTURED" and an American lieutenant explained it to me, I was pale in amazement. How can they say such things about me?'

ERNST KALTENBRUNNER, 4 NOVEMBER 1946

As the indictment party made its way to the next cell, the afternoon light was already fading. They found the occupant half-hidden in shadow – he was a monstrous figure, both in stature and reputation. Ernst Kaltenbrunner was not the type of man one would want to share a cell with. The former head of the Reich Security Office, he was implicated in the torture and murder of countless enemies of the regime – most notably Admiral Canaris, the director of the Military Intelligence Service, who had conspired to assassinate the Führer in 1944. It was Kaltenbrunner who had ordered the Gestapo to resort to torture when Canaris refused to confess.

Kaltenbrunner was volatile, wilful and deceitful – the ideal man for the post. A heavy smoker, he began the day with a couple of glasses of brandy and only became reasonable when he had finished the bottle. His massive frame filled the cell. When he grinned he revealed gaps in his black teeth, but he was not grinning now. He was weeping – just another cornered bully with no thugs to do his dirty work. In the witness box he would repeatedly deny the evidence of his own eyes, refusing to acknowledge the documents that bore his name. He did this so often that he became known as 'the man without a signature'. Now he squirmed, 'sick with fright', as he denied all knowledge of Adolf Eichmann, the architect of the Final Solution, even though he had known him since boyhood and had served alongside him in the SS.

He stopped snivelling for a moment and drew himself up to his full height.

'I refuse to serve as an ersatz for Himmler,' he growled. 'I was a soldier.' Then he relapsed, sobbing. 'Who would defend me? I have no friends.'

By now the strain was beginning to tell on Major Neave. It was a draining and depressing duty he had been given. There was no longer any honour in it.

Ernst Kaltenbrunner (far left) on a visit to Mauthausen concentration camp in Austria in 1941. He is accompanied by (from left to right): Franz Ziereis, the camp commandant; Heinrich Himmler; and August Eigruber, Gauleiter of Upper Austria.

Ley – Slave-driver

Robert Ley had been the leader of the German Labour Front, an organization that took the place of the trade unions, which were outlawed by Hitler when he came to power in 1933. Under the new regime, German workers were forced to work harder and longer and they could not strike or leave their jobs without the government's permission. The Nazis avoided discontent, and reconciled the workers to the regime, by providing a range of subsidized leisure activities, which proved very popular with the German population.

It was Dr Ley's wartime activities that led him to be indicted as a war criminal, particularly his deep involvement in the acquisition and mistreatment of foreign slave workers. Confronted in his cell he ranted at his visitors.

'Why don't you just put us all up against a wall and shoot us?'

He was clearly mentally and emotionally unstable, a condition no doubt exacerbated by his alcoholism. His hysteria, combined with an intermittent vacant expression, troubled Neave, who wondered if he was fit to stand trial on such serious charges. Six days later the question was redundant. On the night of 25 October Ley twisted a wet towel into a makeshift noose and hanged himself in his cell, having first stuffed his underpants into his mouth to stifle his cries.

Colonel Andrus was incandescent with anger. He immediately made sure that each of the cells was put under constant guard. In addition, the guards were ordered to check on the prisoners once every minute.

'I won't let these bastards take the easy way out!' he raged.

Robert Ley saluting Hitler, April 1937. A fanatical supporter of Hitler, Ley last saw him in his Berlin bunker on 20 April 1945, the Führer's birthday.

Sauckel – Slave Trader

'I was given this assignment which I could not refuse – and besides, I did everything possible to treat them well.'

FRITZ SAUCKEL, 23 FEBRUARY 1946

Fritz Sauckel, *Gauleiter* of Thuringia, had acted as Albert Speer's second-in-command. He had supplied him with slave workers – an estimated 10 million from 1942 to the end of the war – who were beaten, starved, brutalized and kept in intolerable conditions. Some were driven to amputate their own hands by placing them in the path of a train, or into machinery, to put an end their misery. The incident would be written off as 'sabotage' by their infuriated Nazi masters.

It is typical of the Nazi mentality that Sauckel denied his part in the workers' maltreatment. He told Dr Gilbert, the prison psychologist, that he had acted merely as an agent when he had been procuring foreign workers for German industrialists such as Krupp and that he had no influence on the conditions in which they were

Sauckel in the witness stand. He claimed to be deeply shocked by revelations of conditions in the labour camps.

kept. He had, he claimed, demanded fair treatment for Russian prisoners and workers, who should have felt that 'it is in their deepest interest to work for Germany'. There was to be 'no unnecessary harshness, rudeness or insults' when dealing with the slaves as it was 'unworthy of the German official and employee'.

His crime was his stupifying naivety and his misplaced loyalty. Sauckel was typical of so many of the petty bureaucrats with whom Hitler surrounded himself – serving the Führer gave his insignificant life some meaning. He was unquestioning in his fanatical devotion to the Führer, whose approval became an addiction. Obedience also prevented him from asking too many questions. Had he done so he would have been horrified. Faced with the indictment, this bald, unimaginative nonentity regarded his accusers with pleading eyes and made a confession in a high-pitched voice.

'The terrible happenings in the concentration camps have shaken me deeply'.

A haggard-looking Albert Speer eats a standing dinner in an improvised dining room for the defendants in the Palace of Justice. Two US military policemen look on.

Speer – Architect of Destruction

'I would like to sit down and write one final blast about the whole damn Nazi mess and mention names and details and let the German people see once and for all what rotten corruption, hypocrisy, and madness the whole system was based on. I would spare no one, including myself.'

ALBERT SPEER, FEBRUARY 1946

Albert Speer, Hitler's architect and minister of armaments, knew the full extent of the Nazi slave labour programme, although he denied doing so under cross-examination. His overly sincere protestations of guilt struck many who attended the trial as merely expedient, as did his subsequent claim to have planned an attempt (conveniently impractical) on Hitler's life. It was all seen as a cynical ploy to portray himself as the 'good German', the repentant Nazi. He claimed to have woken from the nightmare just in time to prevent Hitler from instigating his scorched earth policy, which would have robbed Germany of any chance of regeneration.

It was easier to deal with the SS thugs, the sadistic concentration camp doctors and the fanatically devoted party officials – their loyalties were uncomplicated, their motives were clear and their guilt was self-evident. Speer – tall, dark and distinguished – was a different case. An intellectual and a technocrat, he was capable of concealing his true feelings and motives. He appeared sincere and he presented himself as a man of integrity, but his true motives were hard to define. He claimed that if Hitler had been capable of cultivating friendship, he would have counted himself as the Führer's closest friend – a statement that revealed his capacity for duplicitous double-think and drawing whatever conclusions he considered convenient at the time. The historian Hugh Trevor-Roper considered Speer to be the 'real criminal of Nazi Germany' because he sat in the centre of the web for 10 years and did nothing to influence policy. He professed ignorance of everything that had occurred in the forced labour and concentration camps and dismissed the excesses as extreme political measures that were none of his business.

It was his smooth and patronizing manner that repelled Major Neave on their first meeting. Despite his courage and strength of character, Neave had Speer down as a man who could not be trusted. Like his subordinate Sauckel, Speer had discouraged violence because it was counterproductive, not for any humanitarian reason. He was, of course, flattered by the Führer's patronage, but it was a marriage of convenience. Hitler was not interested in how a task was carried out – he was only concerned with results. This gave Speer the freedom to implement his own ideas regarding armament production, without having to justify his methods. But it was this disregard for the consequences of his actions that brought Speer to trial.

Speer was only 40 years old when he was indicted and he might have been hoping that if he showed sufficient contrition and appeared co-operative he could get away with a lighter sentence. Perhaps he would be able to rehabilitate himself into German society and even profit by his wartime experiences. He regarded Neave with a nervous smile.

'The trial is necessary,' he said in fluent English. He was endeavouring to be polite, pleasant and reasonable under the circumstances. Neave thought him even more beguiling and dangerous than Hitler.

Von Neurath – The Unwise Baron

'Hitler was a liar, of course – that became more and more clear. He simply had no respect for the truth. But nobody recognized it at first...'

KONSTANTIN VON NEURATH, 15 DECEMBER 1945

As the party waited for the guard to locate the key to the next cell, distant piano music drifted across from a room in the palace. It was a poignant reminder of the world in which the next defendant had once lived. Now 73 years old, Baron Konstantin von Neurath was an upper-class diplomat who had unwisely accepted the posts of Hitler's foreign minister and Reichsprotektor in Czechoslovakia. Common sense should have told him that he was being used to legitimize an unprincipled administration, but the baron was not the brightest card in the pack. His manners might have been impeccable and his pedigree unimpeachable but he had a weak, affable personality which made him a perfect foil for the unscrupulous dictator.

A Hitler dupe, von Neurath rubber-stamped the repression of the Czech people.

He appeared dressed in a grey striped suit, the very picture of respectability, in stark contrast to the picture painted by the indictment, which charged him with rubber-stamping the repression of the Czech people and other actions to which he had never raised an objection. Hitler was nothing if not a good judge of character. He knew how to pick his henchmen and not all of them had worn jackboots.

The baron's complacency was offensive. The indictment party left him to ponder his part in the whole sordid affair.

Von Papen – The Silver Fox

'I think [Hitler] wanted the best for Germany at the beginning, but he became an unreasoning evil force with the flattery of his followers – Himmler, Goering, Ribbentrop, etc. ... I tried to persuade him he was wrong in his anti-Jewish policies many a time. He seemed to listen at first, but later on, I had no influence on him.'

FRANZ VON PAPEN, 30 OCTOBER 1945

Franz von Papen acquired the appellation 'The Silver Fox' on account of his silver hair and his vulpine features, although he lacked cunning and was considered to be a dilettante by Hitler's inner circle. He liked to think of himself as a spymaster, but when he served as a military attaché to the German ambassador in Washington during the First World War he committed so many blunders that he deserved to be imprisoned for incompetence, if nothing else. As one embarrassing episode followed another he laughed it all off as a 'tremendous sensation', but his own people were not fooled and few found the exposure and the imprisonment of their agents to be funny. German naval officer Captain von Rintelen called von Papen a 'foolish and stupid intriguer', but Hitler never considered that incompetence was a reason for disqualifying someone he liked from high office.

On his accession to power in January 1933, Hitler made von Papen his vice-chancellor. It was his way of appeasing President von Hindenburg, who was known to despise the 'jumped-up Bavarian corporal'. When Papen became vice-chancellor he made a promise to the ageing president.

'In two months we shall have Hitler squeezed into a corner so that he squeaks.'

Hitler knew full well what von Papen had said, but he paid little heed to his subordinate's words.

The French ambassador had sized up von Papen up neatly when he described his character.

'There is something about Papen that prevents either his friends or his enemies from taking him seriously: he bears the stamp of frivolity, he is not a personality of the first rank.'

Von Papen received the indictment with feigned indifference.

'I cannot understand why I find myself in this position, Herr Major,' he remarked, as if accepting a summons for slander. His sense of self-importance seemed undiminished. Perhaps he had been destined to end his ignominious career in jail.

He later declared that he was a man of peace.

'I've been portrayed as an intriguing devil. But I can prove I have always worked for peace... I am confident in American justice, and am glad to have the truth brought to light through this trial.'

It is indicative of von Papen that he subsequently engaged Dr Kubuschok, an advocate as long-winded and incompetent as himself, of whom Justice Birkett remarked that his conspicuous absence of skills was 'a degradation of the arts of advocacy'.

Von Papen's physical features that gained him the moniker 'Silver Fox' are clearly visible in this photograph taken of him in court, but the appearance of deepseated cunning was illusory.

Seyss-Inquart – The Quisling

'The southern German has the imagination and emotionality to subscribe to a fanatic ideology, but he is ordinarily inhibited from excesses by his natural humaneness. The Prussian does not have the imagination to conceive in terms of abstract racial and political theories, but when he is told to do something, he does it.'

ARTHUR SEYSS-INQUART, APRIL 1946

Austrian Arthur Seyss-Inquart was an unrepentant Nazi, a quisling who had sold his own country to the Germans in exchange for power and privilege. He was Reichskommissar of the Netherlands and deputy to the Polish governor-general Hans Frank, but to the end he maintained that he was merely a representative of the administration, who had been given the onerous duty of 'negotiating' the annexation of Austria in March 1938. In truth, he had been the lackey at Hitler's side when the dictator had threatened the Austrian chancellor, Kurt von Schuschnigg, with a military invasion if he did not agree to *Anschluss* (unity with Germany). And it was Seyss-Inquart who had organized the violence that had given Hitler the pretext to march in.

From behind thick glasses this aloof and humourless man surveyed the indictment party with barely suppressed contempt. How dare they judge him? He had only done his duty, had he not, in freeing Austria of the Jews? Why should he be made to feel ashamed of holding the honorary rank of general in the SS? Even after the trial had given him ample reason to question his undying loyalties to the regime, he maintained that he had been measured and reasonable in his treatment of the Dutch civilians. After all, he had ordered that only six hostages be shot for every German killed by the resistance. Other Nazi commissars had demanded ten or more. Did that not show restraint?

At different times, Seyss-Inquart implemented Nazi policy in Austria, Poland and the Netherlands.

He accepted the indictment with a courteous bow and an unattractive smile.

'Last tragic act of the Second World War, I hope?' he asked.

Major Neave declined to take the bait. He was thinking about the 1,200 skilled Dutch diamond-cutters who had been sent to Auschwitz and the 120,000 Dutch civilians who had been transported in cattle trucks to Mauthausen, Sobibor and Belsen, all because of Seyss-Inquart. Their only 'crime' was that they had been born Jewish.

One victim had kept a diary from which the world would learn what it was like to live in daily fear of being discovered and sent to one's death. Her name was Anne Frank. She died in Auschwitz three weeks before her 16th birthday – just two months before Germany surrendered.

Schacht – Hitler's Banker

'All I wanted was to build up Germany industrially... The only thing they can accuse me of is breaking the Versailles Treaty.'

HJALMAR SCHACHT, 11 JANUARY 1945

Dr Hjalmar Schacht was cut from a very different cloth, but he was equally unrepentant. He stubbornly refused to accept that he had played a significant part in oiling the wheels of tyranny. His arrogance and insolence astounded the guards. Perhaps he thought that his time in Dachau, when he had been imprisoned for his opposition to Hitler, might count in his favour. But his protest had not been based on moral grounds. His stand against Hitler had been solely concerned with his leader's fiscal irresponsibility. War would be expensive. Schacht had kept the Nazi party afloat financially after the election defeat of 1932. He had introduced Hitler to leading industrialists, whose support was crucial in the party's subsequent rise to power, and he had no wish to see his work ruined by the Führer's rashness.

But Schacht's loyalty and admiration for his leader's political instincts were undiminished. In March 1938 he addressed his employees.

'No one can find his future with us who is not with a full heart behind Adolf Hitler.'

In the event, he organized a loan to the munitions industry totalling 12 billion marks, by issuing 'Mefo' bills of exchange. This dubious strategy, based on a dummy company, did not adversely affect the money supply and so it did not risk inflation. By such means Schacht became a silent partner in the conspiracy and as such his protestations of innocence sounded as hollow as any made by his fellow defendants.

Schacht glared at Major Neave through his thick glasses. He was tall, with a shock of white hair that was matched by the starched brightness of a high collar he had made out of paper.

'I will read these documents,' he said haughtily, taking a copy of the indictment, 'but of course I expect to be acquitted. I am, after all, a banker.'

Then in a deeply patronizing tone he demanded to see his son-in-law, who was a jurist, as if that would carry any weight with the tribunal. With barely a breath he began to lecture Major Neave on the injustice and the indignity of his position. He had nothing but contempt for his fellow defendants, particularly Kaltenbrunner, who had once questioned Schacht about his part in the July plot, although there was no evidence to suggest he had been anything more than an interested bystander.

By late October Schacht had condescended to be tried.

'I have full confidence in the judges,' he remarked, 'and I am not afraid of the outcome. A few of the defendants are not guilty; most of them are sheer criminals.'

Hjalmar Schacht was a prime mover in the reindustrialization and rearmament of Germany prior to 1939, yet always considered himself wholly innocent of any war crimes.

First and foremost a military man and fierce German patriot, Alfred Jodl would not accept direct responsibility for Nazi atrocities, claiming that he had merely been following orders.

Jodl – Just a Soldier

'The indictment knocked me on the head. First of all, I had no idea at all of about 90 per cent of the accusations in it. The crimes are horrible beyond belief, if they are true. Secondly, I don't see how they can fail to recognize a soldier's obligation to obey orders. That's the code I've lived by all my life.'

ALFRED JODL, 1 NOVEMBER 1945

Colonel-General Alfred Jodl had been chief of operations for the German High Command (OKW) and Hitler's principal military adviser, but when Major Neave faced him for the first time he was standing to attention in carpet slippers, stripped of his epaulettes. On his arrival in Nuremberg, Jodl had protested that he would not be tried with the likes of Streicher because he was a soldier who should be accorded the privileges and respect due to his rank.

Colonel Andrus responded by ripping the epaulettes from his shoulder and reminding him that he was no longer an officer but a war criminal. Jodl was visibly shaken by the insult, but he retained his dignity and remained courteous when he was handed a copy of the indictment.

'Will you advise me, Herr Major, what sort of lawyer I should have to defend me – an expert in criminal law or an expert in International Law?'

It was an intelligent question because he was charged with both war crimes and crimes against humanity. As chief of OKW operations, he had been responsible for planning the domination of Europe, which was a potential war crime. And then he had countersigned orders for the execution of unarmed prisoners of war, which could be seen as a crime against humanity. Throughout all of this he had remained blindly devoted to Hitler, in the belief that he was one of the greatest military minds of all time – but then the Sixth Army's defeat at Stalingrad brought him to his senses. Even so, he remained fiercely loyal, raising no objections to the 'excesses' that followed in the wake of the victorious Wehrmacht. He had not taken the opportunity to burn his personal files when he had the chance because he genuinely believed that Hitler's war was a just war, a 'preventative' war against the creeping sickness of Communism at home and abroad.

His watchword was duty and he had no patience or sympathy for those who needed to consult their conscience before carrying out their orders. Jodl had criticized those of his fellow officers who had questioned Germany's preparedness for war and he was ashamed to wear the same uniform as those who had plotted the Führer's assassination.

But Jodl's most immediate problem was having no paper or pen with which to prepare his defence. The decisive, energetic general staff officer who had coolly planned the German army's invasion of Europe in 1939 was now at a loss for want of a pen.

Keitel – Hitler's Office Manager

'We all believed so much in [Hitler] and we stand to take all the blame – and the shame! He gave us the orders. He kept saying that it was all his responsibility.'

WILHELM KEITEL, 25 DECEMBER 1945

Field Marshal Wilhelm Keitel flushed at the sight of the indictment and hung his head in shame – as well he might, for it was he who had signed the infamous *Kommandobefehl* that had instructed the German army and naval personnel to shoot captured commandos in cold blood. He was universally despised. His guards mocked his unquestioning obedience and lack of backbone – they joked that he would have made a fine first sergeant in the American army – and his fellow officers thought him an insufferable sycophant. Hitler had appointed him chief of staff to the German High Command (OKW) because he would make the ideal 'office manager', they said. His colleagues called him 'Nickesel' behind his back, a reference to a toy donkey that nodded obediently when tapped on the head, while Hitler condemned him for having the brains of a cinema usher. Keitel may have been a dullard, but he was under no illusion that he was installed as a mere functionary.

Keitel in his prison cell, still wearing his uniform, which has been stripped of its epaulettes and insignia.

'How in heaven's name can they accuse me of conspiring to wage aggressive war,' he later complained to the prison psychiatrist Dr Gilbert, 'when I was nothing but the mouthpiece to carry out the Führer's wishes? As Chief of Staff I had no authority whatsoever – no command function – nothing.'

In the cell, stripped of his insignia, he was a disgraced desk soldier whose only defence was that he was obeying orders. It would not be enough to save him from the gallows.

Doenitz – The Last Führer

'Politicians brought the Nazis to power and started the war. They are the ones who brought about these disgusting crimes, and now we have to sit there in the dock with them and share the blame!'

KARL DOENITZ, 27 MAY 1946

In the weeks following the end of the trial, Admirals Doenitz and Raeder received more than one hundred letters of sympathy from American and British naval officers. The Germans' former enemies deplored the verdicts and expressed dismay that such 'honourable men' had been shamed by the association with their Nazi masters, but their sympathy was misplaced. The truth of the matter was that Doenitz was a fervent National Socialist who had stated that his fellow countrymen were 'worms' compared to the Führer. He was charged with waging aggressive war and with war crimes, specifically the failure to rescue enemy sailors from torpedoed ships. Even worse, he ordered survivors to be fired upon as they lay helpless in the sea and in lifeboats – the so called 'Laconia Order' of September 1942.

This uncompromising officer was fiercely proud of the German navy and he had not hesitated to contradict Hitler when he spoke of his admiration for the Royal Navy. But it was the only occasion on which Doenitz had dared to speak against the Führer. At all other times he had been in complete accord with Hitler's fanatical last stand strategy and he was equally indifferent to the suffering of the front-line soldiers. In 1943, having accepted that the war at sea could not be won, he had pulled 50,000 sailors from their posts and sent them into battle on the Russian front, knowing that none of them had combat training. No wonder Hitler named him as his successor in his final testament, entrusting Doenitz with the continuing battle against Bolshevism.

When he was served with the indictment his dull grey eyes flashed.

'With what conspiracy am I charged?' he asked, seething with resentment. 'I waged an honourable war against your country.'

But he had been damned out of his own mouth when he had addressed a group of senior naval officers in February 1944.

'From the very start the whole officer corps must be so indoctrinated that it feels itself co-responsible with the National Socialist state in its entirety. The officer is the exponent of the state. The idle chatter that the officer is non-political is nonsense.'

He might have been a highly competent officer but he was naive, and it was his artlessness, as much as anything, that spared him from a longer prison sentence. He was fortunate to be defended by a brilliant fellow naval officer, Otto Kranzbuehler, who argued that the Laconia Order did not explicitly instruct German U-boat commanders and naval officers to fire on survivors, nor abandon them. They were merely being instructed to make the safety of their own crew and vessels a priority. If remaining in the area put their crew at risk from enemy planes or shipping, their orders were to leave the survivors to their fate. Kranzbuehler successfully argued that the Allies had done the same, which spared Doenitz the indignity of dying with the likes of Gestapo chief Ernst Kaltenbrunner and 'butcher' Hans Frank.

The prisoners had to sweep their cells daily, but Doenitz was obsessively tidy. His pencils and notepad were carefully arranged on the small table, which showed that this was a man in control of both his life and his emotions. He was dressed in a smart blue suit that would have looked well on a school teacher or a provincial doctor, but which seemed somehow unflattering when worn by the former U-boat commander-in-chief. His harsh features betrayed barely repressed anger at having been deprived of his liberty and the authority that he had wielded as admiral and the last Führer of the Third Reich.

Two Faces

His encounter with the 20 defendants reminded Neave that the Nazi elite showed two distinct faces to the world. First there were the cultured, self-serving, pseudo-intellectuals, whose innate anti-Semitism had been made socially acceptable by Hitler. They saw themselves as members of an exclusive club.

And following on behind were the insignificant personalities who maintained the machinery of terror. These officious petty bureaucrats had been elevated to positions that gave them the power of life and death over their fellow citizens.

Both groups were without conscience or compassion and they would change their allegiance as soon as their beloved leader revealed his true nature – that is, his desire for self-destruction. These were hollow men, the superficial ciphers of a tyrannical regime that existed only to enrich itself at the expense of others, an administration that had no vision other than self-glorification and gratification.

The Nazis had made no contribution to culture. Their art and their architecture was bland, derivative, pretentious and entirely without merit; their science sought only to substantiate their own ideological assumptions; their philosophy was perverse; and their racist ideology was abhorrent and inhumane in the extreme.

The Third Reich was destined for self-destruction because it had been formulated by a psychotic mind – the mind of the archetypal *Untermensch*, Adolf Hitler. But for 12 terrible years it had given power to men who were unworthy to wield it, men who now awaited the judgement of the world they had attempted to enslave and destroy.

To their lasting credit, the enemies of the Reich were now willing to give the accused the luxury of a trial. It was something that the defendants would have denied their enemies.

Mastermind of the U-boat 'wolfpack' tactic against Allied convoys in the Battle of the Atlantic, Doenitz regarded himself as a naval man, not a politician, and therefore not guilty of war crimes.

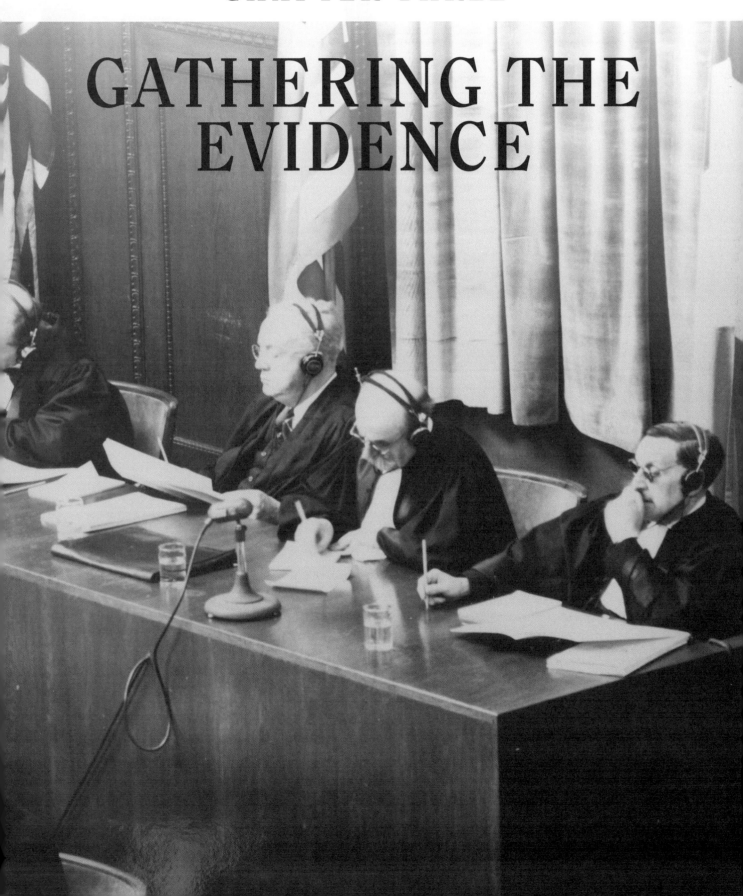

CHAPTER THREE

GATHERING THE EVIDENCE

Fortunately for the prosecution the German reputation for thoroughness and order was taken to an extreme by the Nazi administration. Detailed records of every order, and memos of every meeting, had been kept and dutifully filed. Requisitions for everything from stationery supplies to canisters of Zyklon B gas (used to murder the inmates of the death camps) had been countersigned by those responsible for the implementation of Nazi policy. Many of these documents had been burned in haste as the Allies closed in, but mountains of paperwork survived to be presented in evidence at the tribunal and at subsequent trials. All of this was augmented by excerpts from official decrees, the transcripts of key speeches and correspondence between departmental heads.

As United States Army investigator Benjamin Ferencz remembered:

> 'We would prepare a list of the evidence, proof of what transports had come into the camp, how many people had been registered as being killed on the various dates, the supposed cause of death – which was obviously fictitious, such as "*Auf der Flucht erschossen*," shot while trying to escape… listing some disease page after page.
>
> 'My mind just refused to grasp what my eyes saw, these people who were lying in the dirt – mostly you couldn't tell whether they were dead or alive. They didn't look like human beings, many of them; they looked animal-like, almost. Or like skeletons.'

Prosecutor Whitney Harris was another who was stunned by the abundance of evidence:

> 'I visited many Gestapo offices and I found documents lying around on the floor, saying, "This man should be executed," and I picked them up off the floor. There were many, many documents that were not destroyed that we obtained and were incriminating.'

When Jackson heard what had been found he said:

> 'I did not think men would ever be so foolish as to put in writing some of the things the Germans did… The stupidity and the brutality of it would simply appal you.'

In the following weeks truck-loads of documents arrived at the courthouse to be catalogued, copied and translated. By the time the trial opened several storerooms were packed from floor to ceiling with cartons and crates.

Donald E. Spencer, head of the documents division. The tonnes of documentary evidence brought to Nuremberg from all over Germany and other countries which had been occupied by the Nazis required a dedicated team of archivists, translators and copyists to handle the sheer volume of paperwork.

After consultation with US Army psychologist Dr Gilbert, Colonel Andrus was forced to allow his prisoners a daily period of exercise in the prison exercise yard — always under close guard, of course. The prisoners' faces have been blacked out in this photo.

Cracking the Criminal Mind

There was no shortage of eyewitnesses. Former Nazi officials and concentration camp guards were among those who provided evidence in the hope of receiving a more lenient sentence, but the most damning evidence of all was extracted from the mouths of the accused themselves. Freed from the tyranny of Hitler's personality, and no longer fearful of being denounced as traitors by their enemies within the Nazi regime, several of the defendants opened up to the prison psychiatrists during lengthy interrogations in their cells.

All of the defendants had been formally interrogated at one or the other of two Allied internment camps before arriving at Nuremberg. The first of these camps – code-named 'Dustbin' – was situated at Kransberg Castle, just north of Frankfurt. Many of its inmates had been engaged in industry and finance. The other camp, 'Ashcan' – located at the Palace Hotel in Mondorf-les-Bains, Luxembourg – catered mainly for senior Nazis from Hitler's government and the armed forces. But the transcripts of the interrogations were used mainly for background information, because they did not relate directly to the charges. Of more significance were the informal interviews conducted at Nuremberg by United States Army psychologist Dr Gilbert and his colleagues Dr Kelley and United States Army major Leon Goldensohn.

Colonel Andrus had little use for the services of a 'headshrinker', but when Dr Gilbert pointed out that the colonel had created the perfect 'suicide ward', Andrus was forced to listen.

The prisoners, Gilbert pointed out, had nothing to do all day but ponder their fate. Daily exercise and something to occupy their time might keep them alive. The colonel reluctantly offered a compromise. Dr Gilbert would have unlimited access to the prisoners in exchange for a daily report on their state of mind and intentions. He reminded Dr Gilbert that his charges were prisoners and not patients and that conventional rules pertaining to client-patient privilege did not apply to men who had broken every written law and moral code of conduct. But yes, they would be able to take a daily turn around the exercise yard and they would have access to a small library. It was customary, was it not, to give the condemned man a last request?

Off-the-Record Interviews

None of the defendants interviewed by Dr Goldensohn felt a need to confess their guilt. Even in the privacy of their cells, and after being assured that whatever they said would be off the record, they still denied the charges. Nor would they accept responsibility for the suffering they had caused. Indoctrinated and conditioned by their own propaganda, they found a rationale for everything they had done.

Hitler's former henchmen in the Anglo-American jail for top-ranking Nazis at Mondorf-les-Bains, Luxembourg in November 1945. The group includes Hermann Goering (front, centre); Joachim von Ribbentrop and Walther Funk (second row, from left); as well as Hans Frank, Karl Doenitz, Alfred Jodl, Alfred Rosenberg, Wilhelm Keitel, Wilhelm Frick and Julius Streicher.

Goering

Dr Goldensohn observed that Goering was prone to mood swings. He was also childlike in the way he sought attention – he would willingly have seen his fellow defendants walk free if he could have had the stage all to himself.

> 'Why don't they let me take the blame and dismiss these little fellows – Funk, Fritzsche, Kaltenbrunner? I never heard of most of them until I came to this prison!'

To the psychiatrist's surprise, Goering denied that he was an anti-Semite:

> 'Anti-Semitism played no part in my life... I never had any feeling of hatred toward the Jews. I realize that [statement] looks stupid – that it is hard to understand how a person like myself who made anti-Semitic speeches and who participated as number two man in a regime that exterminated 5 million Jews can say that he was not anti-Semitic. But it is true.'

This was probably one of the few truthful statements made by Goering during the trial. In private he confided that he did not particularly dislike the Jews – he had even saved one Jewish acquaintance from being sent to a concentration camp. He justified his action by remarking, 'I will decide who is Jewish and who is not!'

But he was not ashamed of having established the camps:

> 'Yes, I frankly admit [the creation of] concentration camps for Communists and other enemies of National Socialism at that time, but certainly not with the idea of killing people or of using them as extermination camps... Certainly, as second man in the state under Hitler, I heard rumours about mass killings of Jews, but I could do nothing about it and I knew that it was useless to investigate these rumours and to find out about them accurately, which would not have been too hard, but I was busy with other things, and if I had found out what was going on regarding the mass murders, it would simply have made me feel bad and I could do very little to prevent it anyway.'

His attitude to murder was particularly disturbing:

> 'I have a conscience and I feel that killing women and children... is not the way of a gentleman. I don't believe that I will go to heaven or hell when I die. I don't believe in the Bible or in a lot of things which religious people think. But I revere women and I think it unsportsmanlike to kill children... I take all the responsibility for what happened in National Socialist Germany but not for the things I knew nothing about, such as the concentration camps and the atrocities.'

Goering seemed proud of having stolen art treasures, as if they had been the prize in a great game:

> 'Of all the charges which have been revealed against me, the so-called looting of art treasures by me has caused me the most anguish. But it was not done in the spirit of looting. I like nice things about me. I didn't want them for myself in the final analysis anyway. They would have gone to the museums of Germany for posterity. If I had not taken them they would be in the hands of those damn Russians for the most part.'

Kaltenbrunner

Gestapo chief Ernst Kaltenbrunner put on a very different performance for the psychiatrist – one that was designed to allay the impression that he was capable of the cruelty with which he had been charged. He spoke softly and gave the appearance of being a man in control. Yet Kaltenbrunner's carefully staged act only served to convince Goldensohn that he was capable of ruthlessness.

> 'Do you realize that I learned most about what went on – the atrocities, the concentration camps, the mass murders, the gas chambers, the terrorization of the partisans, and the terrible methods of the police itself against the German people – I learned most about it here, because I only worked in Berlin as chief of the RSHA since 1943... I am thought of as another Himmler. I'm not. The papers make me out as a criminal. I never killed anyone.'

Kaltenbrunner smiled as he said that.

Keitel

Field Marshal Wilhelm Keitel greeted Goldensohn with an ingratiating smile, but his conversation betrayed the fact that he was constantly seeking approval. He was full of sincerity when he addressed the major.

> 'I had no authority. I was field marshal in name only. I had no troops, no authority – only to carry out Hitler's orders. I was bound to him by oath. One of Hitler's prime ideas was that each minister and functionary was to mind his own business. That's why I learned about some of the [war-crime] business for the first time in this court... As for Jewish measures – I tried to keep the army clear of anti-Semitism... What could I do?... I was in it up to my neck by the time I realized the way things were going. What could I do? I could not resign

in time of war; if I refused to obey I would be killed. Or I could commit suicide... But had I taken my life, I wouldn't have improved things, because this demon went ahead with whatever he wanted and succeeded.'

Funk

Walther Funk's vacuous personality posed a problem for the psychiatrist, who found it difficult to analyze a man who appeared to have no thoughts of his own, but simply repeated platitudes and became emotional when asked about politics or his past. His reflexive response to being pressed on more serious matters was always the same.

'I was only a small man and I had no idea of what was going on... Some of my closest friends were Jews... I had many Jewish friends, socially and in business. I never adhered to any racial theory. I thought, as did so many others, at first that the anti-Semitism of the Nazis was [only] a political point... I did not foresee the mass murders or the extermination programmes. Furthermore I personally assisted many Jews who would have been excluded from economic or cultural life... I am guilty of one thing – that I should have cleared out and not had anything to do with these criminals in the first place. Later, it was too late. I was in it up to my neck. But as for the atrocities, I had not a thing to do with them.'

Von Ribbentrop

Joachim von Ribbentrop appeared agreeable, but it seemed to Dr Goldensohn that the former foreign minister was bearing up under a depression. The dominant and recurrent theme of his conversation was puzzlement as to how he had come to such a predicament. He wondered if Hitler had known of the atrocities. Ribbentrop still regarded the dictator as a 'good man', a vegetarian who was kind to animals and children. He was convinced that Hitler's anti-Semitism was rooted in his belief that the Jews were behind an international conspiracy to bring about war between America and Germany.

'The American Jews and others obviously hated the Nazi regime. They refused to co-operate in preventing President Roosevelt and his brain trust from lending assistance to England. Lend-lease continued and the whole American atmosphere toward Germany was hostile. If only these American bankers had intervened and threatened England, forced her to accept Hitler's peace offer – and we were prepared to make a peace with England in 1940 – all these terrible exterminations of the Jews could have been prevented... I was truly under

Hitler's spell, that cannot be denied... He had terrific power, especially in his eyes... Hitler always, until the end, and even now, had a strange fascination over me.'

Ribbentrop admitted that he had contemplated committing suicide when he was captured, but he now felt compelled to 'face the music'.

'I must accept responsibility even though I had no power as foreign minister because it was a dictator state. [In] my defence... I stand up for the foreign policy of Germany from 1938 to the end, but regarding the atrocities, the actions in domestic politics, or the actions in occupied territories I can take no responsibility.'

He sincerely believed that the German people would always regard the Nuremberg defendants as their leaders and that the trial would later be seen to have been a 'mistake'. If only the Allies would admit that there had been such 'mistakes' on both sides there might be some form of reconciliation. Otherwise the German nation would consider any sentences passed on the Nazi leaders as harsh and they would view their leaders as martyrs.

Crude Nazi propaganda portrayed the English as effete and the Americans as decadent.

Streicher

Julius Streicher, 61 years old at the time of the trial, was given to grimacing and leering as he talked. He screwed up his bulging eyes like a sadistic schoolteacher contemplating the prospect of flogging the sixth form and his low intelligence and lack of understanding of the world emerged when he spoke about his all-consuming obsessions. Dr Goldensohn theorized that Streicher's sexual sadism was probably a projection of his interior conflicts. He exhibited a degree of self-loathing that could well have been connected to his latent homosexuality. Unfortunately, by venting his frustration on others he crudely justified the racial crimes endorsed by the equally psychotic Hitler and Himmler.

'My publication was for a fine purpose. Certain snobs may now look down on it and call it common or even pornographic, but until the end of the war I had Hitler's greatest respect, and *Der Stürmer* had the party's complete support. At our height we had a circulation of 1.5 million. Everybody read *Der Stürmer*, and they must have liked it or they wouldn't have bought it. The aim of *Der Stürmer* was to unite Germans and to awaken them against Jewish influence which might ruin our noble culture... I am absolutely convinced that no one sits on the defendants' bench who wanted these mass murders. The charge that I have something to do with having stirred up the populace by propaganda or by my speeches to commit such atrocities is false... My conscience is as clear as a baby's.'

The Interpreter

Goldensohn's interpreter during these informal exchanges was 21-year-old Howard (Hans) Triest. Born in Munich, he left Germany for a new life when Hitler came to power. As Private Triest he landed on Omaha beach with the United States Infantry Division, two days after D-Day, and by May 1945 he was looking forward to going home. But then he was reassigned to Nuremberg to work as a translator. For seven months he accompanied Major Goldensohn on his daily visits to the cells.

'Leon was a really nice, compassionate man,' Triest remembered. 'He had an air around him that made people feel comfortable about confiding in him.'

But his most memorable encounter was when he stood face to face with Jew-baiter Julius Streicher, who took him aside on one of his visits and asked him if he would look after his personal papers. He feared they might fall into the hands of Jews.

'I can smell a Jew from a mile away,' he boasted. 'I can see it in their face, their eyes, from the way they walk, even the way they sit!'

He told Triest that he could tell he came from a very fine Nordic family, which allowed the GI to enjoy a rare moment of macabre humour.

'He went to the gallows not knowing I was Jewish,' said Triest later.

The young German-American experienced very different emotions when he found himself accompanying Dr Goldensohn to the cell where Rudolf Hoess, the commandant of Auschwitz, was being held temporarily while he testified at Nuremberg. Triest's parents had perished at Auschwitz and here was the man who had ordered their deaths, sitting an arm's length away.

'What should I have done, knifed him?' says Triest, when he was asked how he could have suppressed his instinct for revenge. 'No, it was a tremendous satisfaction to know we had captured him and that he was going to hang. That was a comfort.'

The Judges

T here were eight judges at the tribunal – four principal judges and their
alternates – who shared their duties and responsibilities for the entire ten
months of the proceedings. Lord Justice Geoffrey Lawrence presided, with Justice
Norman Birkett as his British alternate; Francis Biddle, the principal American
judge, was paired with his countryman John J. Parker; the French were represented
by Henri Donnedieu de Vabres and Robert Falco; and the Russian team consisted of

*Seated in the back row are the eight members of the tribunal representing the four main Allied countries: the Soviet Union,
Great Britain, the United States and France.*

Major-General of Jurisprudence Nikitchenko and Lieutenant-Colonel Volchkov.

Lawrence was a paragon of patience. Having served as a gunnery officer in the First World War, he understood that the law governing the conduct of war cannot always be applied rigidly and to the letter when men are under fire. He would be scrupulously fair to all parties, for he knew that the victors were not without blame and that it was all too easy to demonize the defendants. Most importantly, he never lost sight of the fact that the accused were on trial for their lives and in the full glare of the world's press. Any lawyer who attempted to use the stage to his personal advantage, or sought to delay the proceedings, was brought sharply back to reality. In his black frock coat, pinstriped trousers, wing collar and bowler hat, the balding judge embodied the

qualities of the English gentleman and the principle of 'fair play'. By the end of the trial even the German lawyers had come to respect him. In the often impromptu and chaotic atmosphere of the trial, where new rules of international law were being defined from day to day, he brought stability, authority and the quiet certainty that what was being done was right. All of those involved felt confident that the ambiguities of the charter would be clarified so that precedents could be established for the future conduct of such trials.

Sitting to the right of Lawrence was Justice Birkett, a formidable advocate who had been deeply disappointed when he was passed over as tribunal president. At six foot three Birkett loomed over Lawrence like a bird of prey, his sharp beak of a nose adding to the illusion. Lawrence was quiet and affable but he rarely smiled, while his partner was impulsive and good-humoured. The two complemented each other and, most importantly, shared a sense of justice tempered by mercy.

Closed Sessions

In the days following the serving of the indictments, the eight judges met in closed session. Sitting in an ill-lit anteroom of the court, their task was to discuss procedure – not easy when the sound of hammering and sawing was going on in the background. One of the topics they discussed at length, and which aroused much heated debate, was the question of whether the Allies should allow the accused to be represented by Nazi advocates.

The terms of the charter were clear – the prisoners had a right to be defended by counsel of their choice. This did not preclude former Nazi lawyers. The Russians were outraged but they were eventually overruled. Biddle argued convincingly that if former Nazis were prohibited from defending the accused, there might not be enough lawyers left in Germany to speak on their behalf. Very few suitably qualified German lawyers were at first willing to defend representatives of the Gestapo and the SS, but Major Neave appealed to their sense of duty. No doubt they were also tempted by the offer of more comfortable accommodation than they had at present, plus the promise of three square meals a day.

Francis Biddle was a former attorney-general under Roosevelt. Like Birkett, he was bitterly disappointed that he had not been appointed president of the tribunal, but he bore the setback well. With his dark bushy eyebrows and trailing moustache, he looked like a frontier marshal. He sat ramrod straight on the bench with a dour expression and he did not tolerate lawyers or defendants who tried to manipulate or exploit any ambiguity to their advantage.

Parker cut a more avuncular figure and would have made ideal casting for the role of a small town judge in a Frank Capra film. His demeanour was in stark contrast to that of the vindictive Nazi judges who had humiliated the July plotters in this same courtroom in 1944, and he shouted them down when they attempted to defend themselves.

The two French judges were reticent and unassuming. They spoke rarely and were seemingly content to observe and report back to Paris. However, when they did interject it was to ask highly pertinent questions, or untangle a convoluted point of law, and this they did with skill and erudition. Donnedieu de Vabres held the post of law professor in Montpelier and had been drafted in for his knowledge of international law, whereas Falco was an appeal court counsel.

Their Russian counterparts could not have been more different. Nikitchenko and Volchkov sat scowling throughout the entire proceedings. They seemed eager to sink their talons into 'the fascist hyenas' who had ravaged their country. Vice-president of the Soviet Supreme Court, Nikitchenko was a hard drinker, who was allegedly frequently seen drunk in public during the course of the trial. But most of the Russians were heavy drinkers and no one begrudged them the right to try to forget what they had been through. Nikitchenko could be good company, however, when Volchkov was not within earshot. It seemed that Volchkov was not so much his partner as his keeper. It was suspected that he was in the employ of the secret police, because he was the only judge to refuse to chair a preliminary meeting when it was his turn. He excused himself by admitting that he was 'unqualified' to do so.

These were the men who would sit in judgement on the most notorious criminals of the 20th century. One item they failed to agree upon, however, was the question of court attire. The British settled for traditional sombre black gowns while the French embellished their robes with jabots and ruffles. Finally, the Russians chose to appear on the bench in their uniforms, which bristled with the medals that attested to their courage. It was a triumphal unspoken gesture that was not lost on the defendants, who had brought nothing but dishonour to their country.

The tribunal in closed session before the trials began. The men had many important points of law and procedure to discuss, ranging from whether the defendants should be allowed to be defended by former Nazi lawyers to the attire that the judges themselves should wear in court.

CHAPTER FOUR

NAZISM ON TRIAL

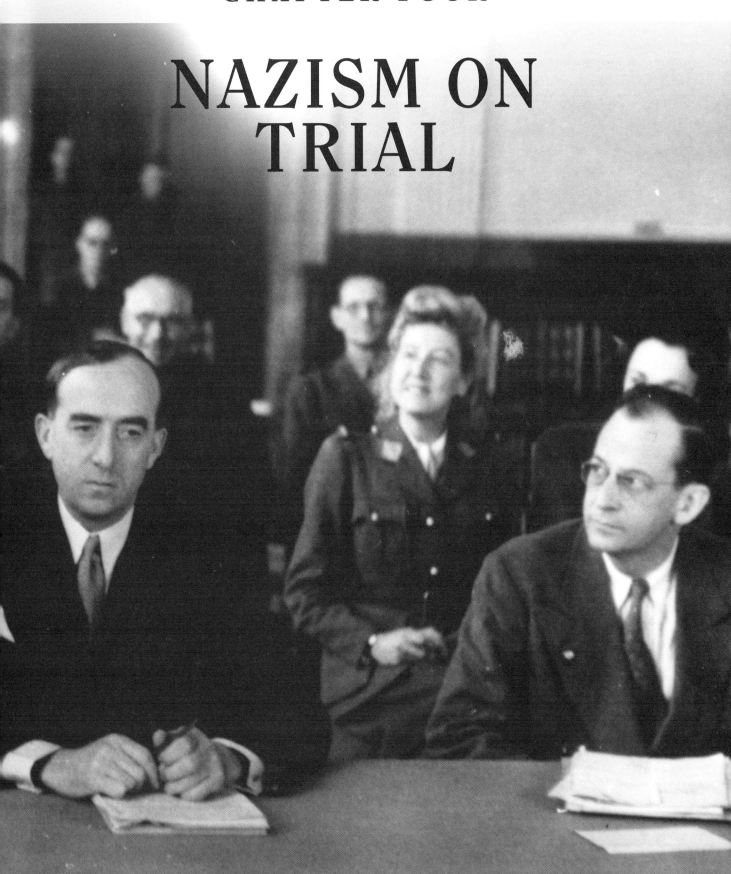

Early on the morning of 20 November, the defendants were escorted from their cells by their guards. They were taken along the covered walkway into the main building before being ushered into the lift that brought them up from the cell block into the floodlit courtroom. The glare of the lights, which had been installed for the benefit of the film cameras, was so strong that the defendants were given sunglasses to shield their eyes. They looked shiftless and decidedly uncomfortable as the judges filed in and the court rose to its feet. There were 20 men in the dock on the first day. Fritzsche and Raeder had been duly delivered from the Russian zone but Kaltenbrunner had been taken to hospital with a suspected subarachnoid haemorrhage. The former Gestapo thug was suffering from acute anxiety – clinically speaking, he was almost frightened to death.

Lord Justice Geoffrey Lawrence (foreground), president of the tribunal, with his colleagues during one of the court sessions. Sustained powers of concentration were required, as the indictments and other documents were dictated into the official court record hour after hour at the start of the trial.

A Catalogue of Crimes

At 10 am, before a hushed and packed courtroom, Justice Lawrence, president of the tribunal, declared proceedings under way.

'This trial which is now to begin is unique in the history of the jurisprudence of the world and of supreme importance to millions of people all over the globe... There is laid upon everybody who takes any part in this trial the solemn responsibility to discharge his duties without fear or favour in accordance with the sacred principles of law and justice.'

There then followed the formal reading of the indictments, which took two days. Each 24,000-word document was read into the official record by junior members of the prosecution, who took it in turn to speak for five hours before handing on to a colleague. It was something of an anticlimax after months of anticipation, but much of the trial would be taken up with monotonous routine, points of procedure and the dictating of reams of documents on which subsequent questions would be based. That said, for anyone who listened carefully there was drama in the indictment, because the full range of Nazi iniquities was detailed in public for the first time. After the main charges of conspiracy were laid out there came references to specific atrocities: the Führer's order for the total destruction of Leningrad, in which one million of its citizens perished; the deportation of civilians; the 'mute evidence of anonymous massacres'; the death of 780 Christian priests at Mauthausen from exhaustion; the execution of civilian hostages in reprisal for acts of sabotage; the destruction of entire communities by the *Einsatzgruppen* in the East; the 400-mile forced march endured by British prisoners of war, who went for 40 hours without food after the fall of Dunkirk; and the murder of 50 RAF officers, who had been recaptured after the 'Great Escape' from Stalag Luft III in 1944.

The only people to be unimpressed by the catalogue of crimes were the perpetrators themselves. Having presumably familiarized themselves with the charges during the long hours of boredom in their cells, they stared blankly ahead as the indictments were read aloud. Hess read a novel or slept and Goering allowed himself the odd chuckle as an inventory of his loot was detailed, but otherwise the men in the dock sat restless and impatient as if they were being forced to listen to a particularly tedious sermon.

View from the Press Gallery

The London *Times* of 21 Nov 1945 reported that the press had outnumbered the defendants and the prosecution on the opening day of the trial and that the prisoners seemed curiously uninterested in the proceedings.

'Looking at them in the dock there was little in their bearing or appearance to suggest that they were on trial for their lives: the enormity of the charges against them involving the deaths of millions of people somehow eluded reality in this unemotional, analytical atmosphere... Goering, far less gross than in the old days, and looking remarkably fit except for the heavy sadness of his eyes, permitted himself a discreet smile at the mention of the million

The trial grabbed the attention of the world's press, who outnumbered the defendants and prosecution teams combined. There was an important principle at stake: justice needs not only to be done but to be seen to be done.

bottles of champagne looted from France, and it was Hess at his side who for the general tenseness of his bearing was constantly to be remarked among the defendants – Hess and the insolent laugh of Hans Frank seated in the middle of the front row.'

Hess was a curious figure. Nobody quite knew what to make of him. He had been glimpsed only briefly in early newsreels prior to his capture in 1941 and afterwards he had been kept in strict isolation. Nuremberg offered the press and the public the first opportunity to view this strange specimen, whom *The Times* described as being 'strained and taut' throughout the proceedings:

'... his dark burning eyes were continually roving about the court when they were not absorbed in a Bavarian novel he had brought into the dock with him, and he smiled cynically when at the outset the batteries of floodlights were switched on overhead for the cameramen operating from an aperture constructed for the purpose high in the walls. Sometimes he engaged Ribbentrop on his left in animated conversation; once he made a remark to Goering, but Goering, chin in hand, and gazing thoughtfully at nothing, ignored him. As for the others, they might almost have been attending some business convention: Dr Schacht has never looked more benign or the chiefs of the German army and navy more Prussian and stolid.'

Jackson's Opening Statement

On the day following the reading of the indictments the defendants were asked to enter their pleas. Goering was first. He rose and opened a folder. He cleared his throat and braced himself for the spotlight.

'I will now read a statement –'

Judge Lawrence cut him short.

'Defendants will not be permitted to make a statement at this time.'

Goering relented, declared himself *'nicht schuldig'* (not guilty) and resumed his seat.

Hess was asked to enter his plea. He stumbled, 'Nein, nein,' which was recorded as 'not guilty' and so it went on as each of the defendants denied the charges for the record.

The pleas having been entered – all 21 defendants declaring themselves 'not guilty' – it was time for Justice Jackson to make his four-hour opening address. At Lawrence's invitation he stepped up to the lectern, opened his notes and began in a measured tone, aware that the world was listening.

'May it please your honours, the privilege of opening the first trial in history for crimes against the peace of the world imposes a grave responsibility. The crimes which we seek to condemn and punish have been so calculated, so malignant and so devastating that civilization cannot tolerate their being ignored because it cannot survive their being repeated. The four great nations, flush with victory and stunned with injury stay the hand of vengeance and voluntarily submit their captive enemies to the judgement of the bar in one of the most significant tributes that power has ever paid to reason. If these men were the first war leaders of a defeated nation to be prosecuted in the name of the law we agree that here they must be given a presumption of innocence and we accept the burden of proving criminal acts and the responsibility of these defendants for their commitment.'

Jackson made it clear that the fate of the individuals in the dock was of no importance to the world, but as symbols of sinister influences they were highly significant. They were the embodiment of racial hatred, rabid nationalism, unfettered militarism, terrorism and the cruellest abuse of power.

'We have no purpose here to incriminate the whole German people. Hitler did not achieve power by a majority vote but seized it by an evil alliance of revolutionaries, reactionaries and militarists. You will hear today and in the days ahead of the enormity and horror of their acts. The prosecution will give you undeniable proofs of these incredible events – and I count myself as one who received during the war most atrocity tales with suspicion or scepticism – no more.

'The catalogue of crimes will omit nothing that can be conceived by their pathological pride, loathing and lust for power. You will hear of the oppression of organized labour, the harassment of the Church, the persecution of the Jews, the conversion of mere anti-Semitism into the deliberate extermination of the Jews of Europe. You will hear of the long series of German aggression and conquests, broken treaties and the terror that settled over Germany, the havoc wrought in the occupied territories and you will know that the real complaining party at your bar is civilization. Civilization asks whether the law is so laggard as to be utterly helpless to deal with crimes of this magnitude by criminals of this order of importance. It doesn't expect that you could make war impossible. It does expect that your judicial action will put the forces of International Law, its precepts, its prohibitions and above all its sanctions on the side of peace so that men and women of good will of all countries may have leave to live by no man's leave underneath the law.'

Drowning in Documents

'I propose today to prove to you that all this organized and vast criminality springs from what I may be allowed to call a crime against the spirit, I mean a doctrine which, denying all spiritual, rational, or moral values by which the nations have tried, for thousands of years, to improve human conditions, aims to plunge humanity back into barbarism, no longer the natural and spontaneous barbarism of primitive nations, but into a diabolical barbarism, conscious of itself and utilizing for its ends all material means put at the disposal of mankind by contemporary science. This sin against the spirit is the original sin of National Socialism from which all crimes spring.'

OPENING STATEMENT BY FRANÇOIS DE MENTHON

After the emotive opening speeches, the coming days and weeks proved something of an anticlimax. The prosecution had decided to divide their case into two phases: the first centring on establishing the criminality of the various arms of the Nazi regime and the second determining the guilt of those arraigned as their representatives. But to prove the former it was necessary to introduce diagrams and documents detailing the structure of Hitler's administration, which was not only uncommonly complex but also exceedingly dull in terms of courtroom drama. Day after day Jackson insisted on reading various documents into the record in order to establish the connection between the various organizations and departments of Hitler's government and to identify who was responsible for the regime's activities. Then he moved on to introduce documentary evidence to support the charge that the administration had collaborated in Hitler's aggression towards Austria. When all of that had been achieved, he repeated the whole process to support the charge of aggressive war against Czechoslovakia, Poland, Denmark, Norway, Belgium, Holland, Luxembourg, Greece, Yugoslavia and the Soviet Union. His thoroughness was admirable but it did not further the prosecution case, it only laid the foundation for it. At one point Jackson was interrupted by Judge Biddle, who pointed out that he had already read eight documents on the subject of manpower initiatives and was it necessary to add another? Jackson answered that it was and then he continued, to the exasperation of the bench and the obvious annoyance of the accused.

By the end of the second week the public gallery had thinned and there were empty seats all round. Goering was heard to joke that he had come to the conclusion that the sentences were already being carried out – Jackson was planning to bore them to death. There was a real danger that the trial was no longer news. Walter Cronkite, journalist and broadcaster, recorded his own view of the proceedings.

'Sitting there for the first time and seeing these twenty one men who had caused such horror in the world I actually felt sick, kind of. They had come into the dock as if this was not a fair proceeding, as if they knew they were going to hang already, why go through this whole thing.'

A young Walter Cronkite, US war correspondent, in the Allied press room of the Palace of Justice. During the war he had been one of eight journalists chosen to fly in bombing raids over Germany.

But finally, the preliminary stage was concluded and the prosecution moved on to the Nazis' use of slave labour and the atrocities perpetrated in the concentration camps. The locations of the major forced labour and extermination camps in Germany and eastern Europe were shown on an annotated map that was displayed on the wall behind the witness stand. In this way the extent of the system of camps could be appreciated by those in attendance.

The prosecution faced a problem however, as United States prosecutor Thomas Dodd explained years later.

'The Nazi conspirators were generally meticulous record keepers, but the records which they kept about concentration camps appeared to have been quite incomplete. Perhaps the character of the records resulted from the indifference which the Nazis felt for the lives of their victims, but occasionally we found a death book or a set of index cards.'

Atrocity Film

The mountain of documents was damning and the testimony of the eyewitnesses would prove extremely credible and persuasive, but words alone would not be sufficient to show the world the true face of Nazism. What was needed was something so shocking, so overwhelming that no amount of posturing and evasion could diminish its impact. United States prosecutor Thomas Dodd found what was needed. Dodd, a former FBI operative, knew the power of photographic evidence and how effective it could be in a criminal trial. Even the smoothest-talking criminals could not dismiss the irrefutable evidence of a photographic image.

At the beginning of the morning session on 29 November, Dodd introduced into evidence film compiled from footage taken by Allied military photographers. It had been taken while their comrades had liberated the areas in which Nazi concentration camps were located. The screening was preceded by the reading of affidavits made by the directors and the cameramen. These attested to the fact that the films were a factual record of what had been found at the camps. They had not been selectively edited or tampered with in any way.

A screen was drawn down behind the witness stand and the lights were doused. Even though brief excerpts from the films had been seen in cinema newsreels throughout the previous year, the assembled audience was still totally unprepared for the cumulative impact of those harrowing images. The first frames showed the network of camps throughout occupied Europe and the sheer number of them elicited a sharp, spontaneous intake of breath from the onlookers. Many had no idea of how extensive the system of death camps had been. An aerial view of Dachau gave way to footage of the gas chambers. Piles of skeletal corpses could be seen, some as high as the blockhouses in which the prisoners had been held. Some appointees turned away, burying their heads in their hands. The stark monochrome images that we are familiar with today were played in rapid succession that morning. All of this took place in complete silence, save for the whirring of the projector and the frequent gasps of disbelief as horror was piled upon horror.

Thomas Dodd, the deputy US chief prosecutor who presented the shocking film evidence from the concentration camps.

Particularly disturbing were the vacant, haunted faces of the human beings who had just been liberated from a hell on earth. They were so shattered in mind, body and spirit that they could not even summon a smile for the camera. It was hard to believe that human beings could have lived through such torment. But many, of course, did not survive the attempt to save them. A single biscuit or a bowl of soup often proved too much for their decimated frames and they died on the day of their liberation.

This victim of Nazi inhumanity still rests in the position in which he died. He was one of more than 1,000 prisoners herded into a barn that was then set alight by SS guards on 13 April 1945, as the US Army advanced, near Gardelegen, Germany.

And then there were the open burial pits at Mauthausen; the wooden sticks wound round with barbed wire which were used to beat the inmates who were too slow to obey orders; the chains which were used to bind prisoners in excruciatingly painful contortions; thumbscrews not seen outside a museum since the Dark Ages: and more corpses, countless white corpses. Some had been shot through the eye, while others had been beaten to death with rifle butts. It was just as well the court was spared the stench the cameramen must have endured, or they would have been sick to their stomachs. And still it went on. The horrified audience saw the faces of people who looked no longer human but more like the ethereal remnants of the living. One old man lay on a stretcher, clasping his hands together as if in prayer. He was thankful to be alive but he had little hope of living to see more than a few weeks or months of freedom. And so it went on.

At Nordhausen captured SS personnel carried wooden planks bearing corpses that looked like broken puppets rather than human beings. The burial pits stretched as far as the eye could see as piles of corpses were crammed in unceremoniously and in great haste, to reduce the risk of an epidemic. There were no grave markers and there was no way of knowing who was being disposed of or even how many corpses there were. The dead were counted in metres.

Then came Belsen. Mounds of skin and bones branded with the camp tattoo were being tossed into trucks to be taken for burial. Female Nazi camp guards who only days before had taunted the inmates and brutalized women and infants now tossed limp bodies into the pits before the bulldozers moved in. The drivers were covering their mouths and noses with handkerchiefs for fear of contamination. It was too much for some. They staggered to the exit and did not return. At last the final frames rattled through the sprockets and the screen went black. The lights came on. Nobody spoke. Not even the judges. They simply rose and went out. The session was adjourned.

Nobody articulated the question that was on everyone's lips.

'How could supposedly civilized people do that to their fellow human beings?'

No one answered because no one knew. There was only incredulity, disbelief and quietly simmering rage.

American broadcaster Walter Cronkite observed the change that came over the court and the accused when the film was shown.

'As soon as the defendants saw the pictures, the film of the concentration camps, they began to wither. As a matter of fact several of them cried. They weren't crying, I don't think, for the Jewish people that were lost. They were crying because they knew that when those pictures were seen in the world they had no way to escape execution.'

Those who still retained a particle of humanity knew that the game was up and that their only hope was to admit their complicity and throw themselves on the mercy of the court. The time for blaming Hitler and the others was passed.

Hess Confesses

The only defendant to remain visibly unmoved by the film was Rudolf Hess.

'I don't understand,' he remarked enigmatically.

Hess had accused the Allies of trying to poison him and in support of his claim he had produced small packets of food which he had brought from Britain. He claimed that the samples contained substances that had caused memory loss and other debilitating ailments. Some members of the prosecution team had no doubt that he was feigning amnesia to escape justice, and a proportion of his fellow defendants shared that view, but there were others who wondered if he was psychologically fit to stand trial for his life. In an effort to kick-start his memory he was shown newsreels in which he had been filmed taking part in Nazi rallies and he was introduced to two of his former secretaries. However, he remained impassive on both occasions. He also failed to recognize Goering when he initially came face to face with him, but he talked animatedly to his fellow prisoner in the dock throughout the days that followed.

The issue had to be decided before the trial could continue and so in the afternoon of 20 November Hess stood alone in the dock as his defence counsel, Dr Gunther von Rohrscheidt, argued that his client was unfit to plead. Afterwards, each of the principal judges gave their expert opinion, as did the prosecution counsel, but before a decision could be reached Hess himself rose and asked to make a formal statement. In contrast to his shambling incoherent former self, he now spoke lucidly and with conviction, making a great impression on those who remained to hear him.

'In order to forestall the possibility of my being pronounced incapable of pleading, in spite of my willingness to take part in further proceedings in order to receive sentence alongside my comrades, I would like to make the following declaration before the tribunal, although I originally decided to make this declaration during a later part of the proceedings:

'Henceforth my memory will again respond to the outside world. The reasons why I simulated loss of memory were tactical. The fact is that only my ability to concentrate is somewhat reduced. However my capacity to follow the trial, to defend myself, to put questions to witnesses, or even to answer questions is not being affected hereby. I emphasize that I bear the full responsibility for everything that I have done or signed as signatory, or co-signatory. My attitude in principle that the tribunal is not competent is not affected by the statement I have just made. So far in conversations with my official defence counsel, I have also simulated loss of memory. He has therefore represented me in good faith.'

The matter seemed settled and on the following day the tribunal ruled that Hess was

*Rudolf Hess (front, centre), Hitler's former deputy in the Nazi party, sits in the defendant's dock next to Hermann Goering.
Standing to the right is Dr Gilbert, the US Army psychologist who had interviewed him.*

capable of standing trial. But his erratic behaviour suggests that he was not mentally fit
and that he was suffering from genuine memory loss for at least some of the time. On
returning to his cell he seemed pleased with his performance. He sought approval from
the prison psychologists Dr Kelley and Dr Gilbert.

'How did I do? Good, wasn't I? I really surprised everybody, don't you think?'

On a subsequent occasion he admitted to Dr Gilbert that the first episodes of
amnesia were genuine but that later he had 'exaggerated somewhat'. After further
formal interrogations Dr Kelley diagnosed the former deputy Führer as a 'self-
perpetuated hysteric'. In the madhouse of Hitler's regime such a man would not have
seemed out of place.

A Strategic Blunder

The court's decision to show the concentration camp images proved to be a turning point in the trial, but another attempt to remind the court of the former lives of the accused backfired badly. Dr Gilbert noticed that when the prosecutors showed a film that celebrated the early victories of the Nazis, including footage of the Nuremberg Rallies, it brought a resurgence of the emotions that were associated with these symbols of power.

The prison psychiatrist immediately observed the prisoners' reactions.

'Even Schacht's eyes were watery as he watched the scenes of reconstruction of Germany after Hitler's rise to power. Later he said to me, "Do you see anything wrong in solving unemployment?" '

Fritzsche said, 'At least it gives me the satisfaction of knowing that there once was a Germany worth working for – up to 1938.'

Ribbentrop was completely overwhelmed by the voice and figure of the Führer. He wept like a baby, as if a dead father had returned to life.

'Can't you feel the terrible strength of his personality? Can't you see how he swept people off their feet? I don't know if you can, but we can feel it. It is *erschütternd!*'

The generals and the admirals gloated as they were shown film of their early victories, and Goering whispered to Hess during scenes of the trials of the July plotters, like an elder brother who wished to bring him up to date on the events he had missed.

The British Set Out Their Stall

On 4 December the British prosecution opened their case with a persuasive speech by Sir Hartley Shawcross, in which he argued that the accused were instruments of Hitler's will and that without their willing participation the tyrant could not have waged his aggressive war. It was these 'broken men' who had planned and initiated the criminal acts carried out in his name. Then with a single thrust the attorney-general made short shrift of the cowardly defence of obeying superior orders.

He observed that a thief cannot escape punishment by claiming that he had only stolen because someone had told him to do so, nor could a murderer walk free because another had commanded him to kill. Loyalty and obedience were fine qualities, but

Sir Hartley Shawcross, chief British prosecutor, at a session in Berlin (the official seat of the tribunal authorities), at which the Allied prosecutors handed over their indictments for the trial.

they were never intended to be exercised without conscience. Almost five hours later he concluded,

> **'And so we believe that this Tribunal, acting, as we know it will act notwithstanding its appointment by the victorious powers, with complete and judicial objectivity, will provide a contemporary touchstone and an authoritative and impartial record to which future historians may turn for truth, and future politicians for warning. From this record shall future generations know not only what our generation suffered, but also that our suffering was the result of crimes, crimes against the laws of peoples which the peoples of the world upheld and will continue in the future to uphold – to uphold by international co-operation, not based merely on military alliances, but grounded, and firmly grounded, in the rule of law.'**

Unfortunately, his duties as attorney-general required Shawcross to be present in Parliament for much of the trial, but he was more than ably succeeded by Sir David Maxwell-Fyfe. A dour and forthright Scot, Sir David proved more than a match for the pompous and patronizing Nazi officials. He had done his homework thoroughly and he had a good eye for detail, which proved crucial when confronted with the defendants' favourite tactic of equivocation, evasion and convenient lapses of memory.

He was ably assisted by barrister G.D. Roberts and four junior barristers, who shared the burden of presenting the evidence on behalf of the British prosecution for the entire 284-day procedure. But those who attended needed more than physical stamina and commitment to justice to get them through some of the proceedings. They also needed a strong stomach.

Gruesome Exhibits

On 13 December Thomas Dodd wheeled in a small table covered in a white sheet and asked for it to be introduced into evidence as Exhibit 253. After a brief introduction he whipped the sheet away to reveal the shrunken head of a Polish prisoner, which had been used as a paperweight by the wife of the commandant of Buchenwald concentration camp. There was an audible gasp in the court. His next exhibit was no less shocking – a piece of tattooed skin flayed from the body of a prisoner for the commandant's wife, who was known to take perverse pleasure in boasting that she had lampshades fashioned from human skin.

Dodd's son later defended his father's melodramatic tactics:

'When we are talking statistics nobody pays much attention, but if I can show you one person who gets murdered you're more apt to pay attention to that. And my father by boiling this stuff down to, in that particular case, one of the atrocities, one individual... If I talked about thousands who lost their lives in Buchenwald, your eyes might glaze over. I hold this up in my hand and say, "This is what happened," even for a seasoned judge it's hard to ignore that.'

But it was evidently not enough to move the defendants to admit their part in these atrocities.

'It would be relieving to hear one of them admit some blame for something,' Dodd wrote to his wife. 'They blame everything on the dead or the missing.'

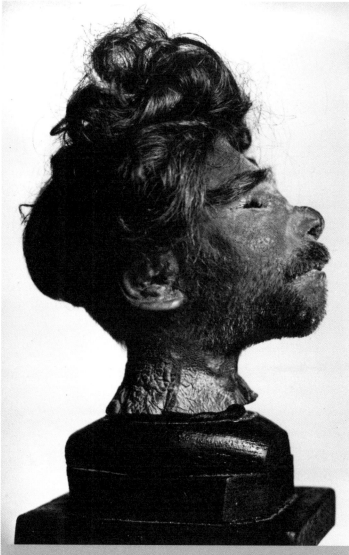

The gruesome shrunken-head paperweight used by Ilse Koch, wife of Buchenwald concentration camp's first commandant. She was known as 'the witch of Buchenwald'.

Criminal Organizations

On 18 December 1945 the prosecution began introducing evidence that would establish the criminality of the various branches of the Nazi regime. This included an affidavit dictated by Dr Sigmund Rascher, who admitted conducting experiments on inmates at Dachau concentration camp. Rascher's affidavit described an experiment that had been designed to determine how best to resuscitate Luftwaffe pilots shot down over the North Sea. Often the pilots would survive the freezing waters only to die later of hypothermia.

Rascher made naked prisoners get into tanks of freezing water to which were added large pieces of ice. Trustees monitored their body temperature and when they were almost dead they were taken out. Various revival methods were then tried out, such as immersing them in tanks of hot or warm water or placing them next to naked female prisoners in the belief that they might respond to 'animal warmth'. If they survived the ordeal they were frequently subjected to the freezing waters once again, after which an alternative method of reviving them was attempted. Rascher noted that most of the inmates went into convulsions and died.

Such cases of unquestionable guilt were offset by doubts regarding the concept of collective guilt. This became a thorny legal topic after the tribunal had declared the six named Nazi organizations to be criminal in nature. Did this mean that every individual member of the German General Staff and the Corps of Political Leaders would be prosecuted? To everyone's relief, this dilemma was resolved when the tribunal ruled that membership alone did not provide grounds for indictment. The organizations themselves were on trial and selected representatives would be summoned to speak on their behalf. To the consternation of the Allied authorities, hundreds of thousands of former members of the SA, the SS and the Leadership Corps responded to the radio appeals, newspaper notices and leaflets distributed all over Germany. By the end of the year 136,000 affidavits from former members of the SS and their representatives had been received and filed. It was clear that die-hard Nazis and Nazi lawyers in the internment camps planned to swamp the Allied War Crimes Commission with paperwork. But the Commission was not to be thwarted or made a fool of. In the spring of 1946 it made arrangements for the defence counsel to visit 80 internment camps throughout Germany. Statements were taken and more than 600 witnesses were selected, from which a final and manageable selection was made. That number was whittled down to 22 by the end of the trial.

The defence case was based on the claim that many members had been compelled to join the indicted organizations under threat of physical violence or imprisonment. When it was clear that this was patently untrue, the argument was widened to include the threat of psychological and financial penalties. It was asserted that individuals had joined because they either feared being out of step with their neighbours or they feared for their businesses or careers. But the tribunal ruled that only the explicit threat of physical compulsion was admissible as a valid defence.

Of the six indicted organizations, only the General Staff and Hitler's brown-shirted bodyguards, the SA, were subsequently acquitted. The SA had dwindled into insignificance after the Röhm purge of 1934, though history still condemns the institution for its part in the persecution of the Jews, before the SS killing squads took over.

Still drowning in documents. This photograph, taken on 30 September 1946, shows the room where the summary of the tribunal and its verdicts was assembled after being mimeographed.

The Little Caesars

The sheer unmitigated gall of some of the witnesses beggared belief. The *Gauleiters* and their subordinates, the *Kreisleiters* and the *Ortsgruppenleiters*, attempted to whitewash their organizations by blaming Hitler, Hess and Bormann for all of their alleged crimes, while the local block and cell leaders, who had acted as informers, tried to convince a subsidiary tribunal that they had performed only 'social and welfare' duties. No one in Germany, it seemed, had been a Nazi. Hitler and Goering had invaded Poland on their own while Goebbels and Himmler had suppressed an entire nation through the power of their personalities. The lie was as sickening as it was transparently untrue.

These provincial 'Caesars' were followed by 12 witnesses for the Gestapo, who testified under oath that the Nazis' most feared organization had been nothing more than the regular state police force, whose duties had extended to 'counter-intelligence work'. However, the witnesses agreed that the Gestapo had been empowered to detain political opponents under 'protective custody'. This innocuous term had struck terror into entire communities and not only in the occupied territories. Many Germans, too, had feared the 'Night and Fog' decree, which gave the Gestapo the right to break into any citizen's home at any time of the day or night and drag them off for questioning, torture and imprisonment without trial. Large numbers of detainees were never seen again. They, too, deserved a hearing and the right to have their persecutors accused in open court.

The tribunal was at a loss for words when one witness stated that the Gestapo were charged with looking after the welfare of families whose male members had been taken into custody, while another stated that the SD (Security Service) 'only dealt with Jewish problems in an advisory and research capacity'. Unfortunately for those witnesses their chief interrogator was none other than Major Airey Neave, whose own experiences at the hands of the Gestapo had led him to believe otherwise. It was the flagrant dishonesty of these witnesses that led the Allied

Nine captured members of the Gestapo. Claims by Gestapo witnesses that they worked only in 'welfare' or 'research' duties sickened the prosecution.

interrogators to despair, but there were even more sickening statements to come.

On 3 January 1946, prosecutors called SS officer Dieter Wisliceny, who testified that he had helped organize the deportation of Jews to extermination camps under Goering's direct orders. Prosecutor Colonel Smith W. Brookhart Jnr asked him what had become of the 450,000 Jews he had rounded up.

'They were all brought to Auschwitz and were part of the final solution,' Wisliceny replied.

'You mean they were killed?'

'Yes, except for about 25 to 30 per cent, that were used for labour purposes.'

Goering was incensed that a German officer had implicated him in the murder of almost half a million civilians.

'It is sickening,' he barked, 'to see how Germans sell their souls to the enemy.'

The case against Goering was gathering momentum.

Dieter Wisliceny, a 34-year-old SS group leader and 'specialist in Jewish matters' from 1940 to 1944, gives his testimony for the prosecution in which he employs the euphemistic term 'final solution'.

A Fate Worse Than Death

'When one sees children [...] in this horrible place [Auschwitz] and the clothes of infants who were killed, it is worth a year of our lives to help to register forever and with practical result the reasoned horror of humanity.'

DAVID MAXWELL-FYFE, BRITISH DEPUTY CHIEF PROSECUTOR, PRIVATE LETTER, 1946

In January 1946, the dead finally found their voice through the testimony of a number of eyewitnesses, who had survived the camps and yet had found the strength and courage to relive their ordeals only yards away from those responsible for their suffering. Marie-Claude Vaillant-Couturier, a former member of the French resistance, recalled under oath what she had seen and heard in Auschwitz on her arrival in 1943. She had been sent there after refusing to sign a false confession. After she had told her interrogator, a German officer, that she was quite prepared to be shot, he had replied that they had means at their disposal which were 'far worse than being shot'. Soon afterwards she found herself herded on to a sealed railway train with 230 other French women. They were given no food or water during the long and terrible journey to Poland. At the end of the line they were separated into two groups – those capable of being worked to death and those selected to die immediately.

Mme Vaillant-Couturier began her statement:

'We saw the unsealing of the cars and the soldiers letting men, women, and children out of them. We then witnessed heart-rending scenes: old couples forced to part from each other, mothers made to abandon their young daughters, since the latter were sent to the camp, whereas mothers and children were sent to the gas chambers. All these people were unaware of the fate awaiting them. They were merely upset at being separated, but they did not know that they were going to their death. To render their welcome more pleasant at this time – June to July 1944 – an orchestra composed of internees, all young and pretty girls dressed in little white blouses and navy blue skirts, played during the selection, at the arrival of the trains, gay tunes such as "The Merry Widow," the "Barcarolle" from *The Tales of Hoffman*, and so forth. They were then informed that this was a labour camp and since they were not brought into the camp they saw only the small platform surrounded by flowering plants. Naturally, they could not realize what was in store for them. Those selected for the gas chamber, that is, the old people, mothers, and children, were escorted to a red-brick building.'

Charles Dubost asked Mme Vaillant-Couturier if these new prisoners were tattooed with an identification number such as the one that had been branded on her arm, but she answered that they were not even counted. They were merely herded like cattle towards the red brick building, which bore the sign *'Baden'* (Baths).

> 'There, to begin with, they were made to undress and given a towel before they went into the so-called shower room. Later on, at the time of the large convoys from Hungary, they had no more time left to play-act or to pretend; they were brutally undressed.'

Mme Vaillant-Couturier stated that she knew this to be the case because she had heard it from a young Jewess called 'Little Marie', whom she had known in Paris.

> 'She was the only one, the sole survivor of a family of nine. Her mother and her seven brothers and sisters had been gassed on arrival. When I met her she was employed to undress the babies before they were taken into the gas chamber. Once the people were undressed they took them into a room, which was somewhat like a shower room, and gas capsules were thrown through an opening in the ceiling. An SS man would watch the effect produced through a porthole. At the end of 5 or 7 minutes, when the gas had completed its work, he gave the signal to open the doors; and men with gas masks – they too were internees – went into the room and removed the corpses. They told us that the internees must have suffered before dying, because they were closely clinging to one another and it was very difficult to separate them.
>
> 'After that a special squad would come to pull out gold teeth and dentures; and again, when the bodies had been reduced to ashes, they would sift them in an attempt to recover the gold.
>
> 'At Auschwitz there were eight crematories but, as from 1944, these proved insufficient. The SS had large pits dug by the internees, where they put branches, sprinkled with gasoline, which they set on fire. Then they threw the corpses into the pits. From our block we could see after about three-quarters of an hour or an hour after the arrival of a convoy, large flames coming from the crematory, and the sky was lit up by the burning pits.
>
> 'One night we were awakened by terrifying cries. And we discovered, on the following day, from the men working in the Sonderkommando – the Gas Kommando – that on the preceding day, the gas supply having run out, they had thrown the children into the furnaces alive.'

There were audible gasps in the court and some of the women could be heard sobbing. Dubost pressed on.

Marie-Claude Vaillant-Couturier (photographed in 1951), French Resistance fighter, former inmate of Auschwitz – where she had been a member of the international clandestine resistance committee for the camp – and brave witness for the prosecution. After the war she was awarded the Légion d'honneur and had a long and successful career in politics as a member of the French Communist Party.

A Cruel Deception

sked to describe what she had witnessed at Auschwitz in the winter of 1943, Mme Vaillant-Couturier recalled that she had seen naked women piled on to open trucks to be taken to the gas chamber. As they were driven away crying and screaming, for by this time they knew their fate, the infamous Ustuf Hessler ran after them beating them with a big stick. Some attempted to escape and were killed on the spot.

The main gate to Auschwitz I. The inscription reads, 'Arbeit Macht Frei' (Work Makes Free). The sign was made by inmates on the camp's metalworkers' labour detail; they deliberately turned the letter 'B' upside down as a clandestine act of disobedience.

The Germans had told the families who were to be taken to Auschwitz that they were going to a ghetto and they should bring all their belongings with them, which included their valuables, which were taken from them on arrival. But the cruellest trick of all was reserved for the Jews from Salonika.

Mme Vaillant-Couturier continued with her testimony.

'I remember that on their arrival they were given picture postcards bearing the post office address of Waldsee, a place which did not exist; and a printed text to be sent to their families, stating, "We are doing very well here; we have work and we are well treated. We await your arrival." I myself saw the cards in question; and the *Schreiberinnen*, that is, the secretaries of the block, were instructed to distribute them among the internees in order to post them to their families. I know that whole families arrived as a result of these postcards.'

Mme Vaillant-Couturier was then subjected to cross-examination by Dr Hanns Marx, attorney to Julius Streicher.

MARX: 'How do you explain that you yourself came through these experiences so well and are now in such a good state of health?'

VAILLANT-COUTURIER: 'First of all, I was liberated a year ago; and in a year one has time to recover. Secondly, I was 10 months in quarantine for typhus and I had the great luck not to die of exanthematic typhus, although I had it and was ill for 3½ months. Also, in the last months at Ravensbrück, as I knew German, I worked on the "Revier" roll-call, which explains why I did not have to work quite so hard or to suffer from the inclemency of the weather. On the other hand, out of 230 of us only 49 from my convoy returned alive; and we were only 52 at the end of 4 months. I had the great fortune to return.'

Marx attempted to cast doubt on the validity of Mme Vaillant-Couturier's testimony by implying that it was all hearsay, to which the witness answered that the major part of her evidence was based on personal experience and the rest could be verified by others who had seen and heard the same things.

Marx was not, however, to be deterred. How could she explain, for example, her very precise statistical knowledge, such as the assertion that 700,000 Jews had arrived from Hungary?

VAILLANT-COUTURIER: 'I told you that I have worked in the offices; and where Auschwitz was concerned, I was a friend of the secretary [the *Oberaufseherin*], whose name and address I gave to the Tribunal.'

MARX: 'It has been stated that only 350,000 Jews came from Hungary,

Eight members of the French communist urban guerilla resistance group Franc Tireurs Partisans-Main d'Oeuvre Immigré line up for a German firing squad, 21 February 1944, Paris. Many resistance fighters ended up in the death camps.

according to the testimony of the Chief of the Gestapo, Eichmann.'

VAILLANT-COUTURIER: 'I am not going to argue with the Gestapo. I have good reasons to know that what the Gestapo states is not always true.'

MARX: 'You said before that the German people must have known of the happenings in Auschwitz. What are your grounds for this statement?'

VAILLANT-COUTURIER: 'I have already told you. To begin with there was the fact that when we left, the Lorraine soldiers of the Wehrmacht who were taking us to Auschwitz said to us, "If you knew where you were going, you would not be in such a hurry to get there." Then there was the fact that the German women who came out of quarantine to go to work in German factories knew of these events, and they all said that they would speak about them outside.

'Further, the fact that in all the factories where the *Häftlinge* [internees] worked they were in contact with the German civilians, as also were the *Aufseherinnen* [female guards], who were in touch with their friends and families and often told them what they had seen.'

Marx concluded his cross-examination with one more cynical attempt to rescue the reputation of the German soldiers.

MARX: 'Up to 1942 you were able to observe the behaviour of the German soldiers in Paris. Did not these German soldiers behave well throughout and did they not pay for what they took?'

VAILLANT-COUTURIER: 'I have not the least idea whether they paid or not for what they requisitioned. As for their good behaviour, too many of my friends were shot or massacred for me not to differ with you.'

The witness was excused.

Dr Hanns Marx (left), attorney to Julius Streicher, and once a member of the Nazi party himself. Streicher was not happy with Marx and asked for him to be taken off the case. Request denied.

Einsatzgruppen – Death Squads

The Russians, too, had their share of atrocity stories. One particularly harrowing example concerned the activities of the *Einsatzgruppen* or SS death squads, in Vilna, west Russia. On 27 February the Russian prosecutor L.N. Smirnov called former local resident Abram Suzkever to the stand to describe what he had seen during the German occupation.

Theodor Eicke (right), commander of the SS-Totenkopfverbande (Death's Head Units), receives the Ritterkreuz (Knight's Cross) somewhere on the Eastern Front during the German invasion of the Soviet Union in 1941. He was involved in the establishment and organization of the concentration-camp system from as early as 1933.

'When the Germans seized my city, Vilna, about 80,000 Jews lived in the town. Immediately the so-called *Sonderkommando* was set up at 12 Vilenskaia Street, under the command of Schweichenberg and Martin Weiss. The man-hunters of the *Sonderkommandos*, or as the Jews called them, the *"Khapun,"* broke into the Jewish houses at any time of day or night, dragged away the men, instructing them to take a piece of soap and a towel, and herded them into certain buildings near the village of Ponari, about eight kilometres from Vilna. From there hardly one returned. When the Jews found out that their kin were not coming back, a large part of the population went into hiding. However, the Germans tracked them with police dogs. Many were found, and any who were averse to going with them were shot on the spot. I have to say that the Germans declared that they were exterminating the Jewish race as though legally.'

In July 1941 all Jews were ordered to sew a yellow Star of David on to their clothes, one on the chest and another on the back, to distinguish them from the other inhabitants. Suzkever stated that those who refused to wear this sign, or who claimed they had not heard of the order, were immediately arrested and were never seen again. The Germans believed themselves to be the master race and they enjoyed humiliating the Jews and Slavs, whom they considered to be *Untermenschen* (subhumans), who existed to serve as their slaves. Suzkever experienced this indignity himself in August 1941.

'A German seized me in the Dokumenskaia Street. I was then going to visit my mother. The German said to me, "Come with me, you will act in the circus." As I went along I saw that another German was driving along an old Jew, the old rabbi of this street, Kassel, and a third German was holding a young boy. When we reached the old synagogue on this street I saw that wood was piled up there in the shape of a pyramid. A German drew out his revolver and told us to take off our clothes. When we were naked, he lit a match and set fire to this stack of wood. Then another German brought out of the synagogue three scrolls of the Torah, gave them to us, and told us to dance around this bonfire and sing Russian songs. Behind us stood the three Germans; with their bayonets they forced us towards the fire and laughed. When we were almost unconscious, they left.'

Escape

That same month the Germans surrounded the old Jewish quarter of Vilna, where up to 10,000 Jews were living. Suzkever was lying in bed ill when he felt the sting of a whip. He jumped up to see Schweichenberg standing over him, a large dog straining at its leash. He was lashing out with the whip and ordering everybody out into the courtyard. There he had the *Sonderkommando* surround the crowd, which was composed of men, women, children, the elderly and the infirm. He told them that they were going to be taken to the ghetto. But the real destination was Lutishcheva Prison where they were to be murdered. At the prison gates they were met by a gauntlet of German soldiers, who beat them with sticks. It was there that Suzkever made his desperate escape, swimming across the Vilia river to take refuge in his mother's house.

Just after dawn on 6 September a large detachment of German soldiers, several thousand in total, surrounded the whole town. Under the direction of Finks, the district commissar, they broke into the Jewish houses and forced the inhabitants into the street. The Jews were then driven to the ghetto. From his hiding place Suzkever saw the Germans rounding up sick Jews from the hospitals, all still in their hospital gowns, in order to parade them before German newsreel cameras.

Not all of Vilna's Jewish population were driven into the two ghettos that Finks had set up. Half of them had been exterminated before the ghetto was established and many others were shot on the forced march through the town.

When Suzkever arrived at the ghetto he witnessed the shooting of an 11-year-old girl, Gitele Tarlo, by Martin Weiss. Suzkever described the restrictions that had been placed on the Jews.

'I must state that the Germans organized the ghetto only to exterminate the Jewish population with greater ease. The head of the ghetto was the expert on Jewish questions, Muhrer, and he issued a series of mad orders. For instance, Jews were forbidden to wear watches. The Jews could not pray in the ghetto. When a German passed by, they had to take off their hats but were not allowed to look at him... At the end of December 1941 an order was issued in the ghetto which stated that the Jewish women must not bear children.'

Soviet prosecutor Smirnov interjected at this point. He asked Suzkever to provide the court with more details of this order.

Slaughter of the Innocents

Suzkever proceeded with his testimony.

'Muhrer came to the hospital in Street Number 6 and said that an order had come from Berlin to the effect that Jewish women should not bear children and that if the Germans found out that a Jewish woman had given birth, the child would be exterminated. Towards the end of December in the ghetto my wife gave birth to a child, a boy. I was not in the ghetto at that time, having escaped from one of these so-called "actions". When I came to the ghetto later I found that my wife had had a baby in a ghetto hospital. But I saw the hospital surrounded by Germans and a black car standing before the door. Schweichenberg was standing near the car, and the hunters of the *Sonderkommando* were dragging sick and old people out of the hospital and throwing them like logs into the truck. Among them I saw the well-known Jewish writer and editor, Grodnensky, who was also dragged and dumped into this truck.

'In the evening when the Germans had left, I went to the hospital and found my wife in tears. It seems that when she had her baby, the Jewish doctors of the hospital had already received the order that Jewish women must not give birth; and they had hidden the baby, together with other newborn children, in one of the rooms. But when this commission with Muhrer came to the hospital, they heard the cries of the babies. They broke open the door and entered the room. When my wife heard that the door had been broken, she immediately got up and ran to see what was happening to the child. She saw one German holding the baby and smearing something under its nose. Afterwards he threw it on the bed and laughed. When my wife picked up the child, there was something black under his nose. When I arrived at the hospital, I saw that my baby was dead. He was still warm...

'Shortly afterwards the second ghetto was liquidated, and the German newspaper in Vilna announced that the Jews from this district had died of an epidemic...'

Of the 80,000 Jews who had lived in Vilna before the German occupation only about 600 remained at the war's end.

Goering Takes the Stand

'Goering knows his goose is cooked and needs a retinue of at least 20 lesser heroes for his grand entrance into Valhalla.'

ALBERT SPEER, JANUARY 1946

At the beginning of March the prosecution case rested and the defence began in earnest. Ironically it lasted longer than the prosecution proceedings, but then there was so much to deny. When the time came to prepare their cases, the defence lawyers were given every assistance by the court. However, they were hampered by the fact that they were entirely dependent on the prosecution when it came to procuring copies of documents, so they were always one step behind. They were also, in most cases, intimidated by the German press, in which they were portrayed as former Nazis, or at least sympathizers. Many, however, were merely fulfilling their professional obligation to represent their clients to the best of their ability, regardless of their personal feelings, and they were given a free hand to do so. Justice Lawrence made things easier for them by censuring the German press for their vitriolic attacks. Buoyed by this gesture, Dr Stahmer, the lawyer representing Hermann Goering, opened his case in a dynamic and hearty fashion. This showed the court that he intended to make a fight of it.

When Goering was called at 2.30 pm on 13 March, he asserted that all he had done was to serve the best interests of the Fatherland.

Walter Cronkite recalls the moment:

Otto Stahmer addresses the court. He was head of the Kriegsmarine Legal Department at the Naval Shipyard, Kiel. Goering chose him from a list of four possible defence attorneys.

'He was arrogant, considerably arrogant. There was no attempt to placate the courtroom. He was telling his story his way, and of course in telling the story he was justifying what had happened as best he could.

Goering in the witness stand testifying on his own behalf. He came across as vain, arrogant, charismatic and supremely sensitive to criticism.

Pretty hard to justify that, but he was skipping over the worst, and defending the need for the Third Reich at the time it came.'

Interpreter Siegfried Ramler found Goering an impressive if repugnant character:

'If one can speak of a dominant personality in the dock, Hermann Goering definitely fits that description as the leading defendant... From the very beginning of the trial he took it on himself to direct the strategy of his co-defendants by sending notes from the dock to various defence lawyers with suggestions of issues to be raised, questions to be asked, and witnesses to be called. This manipulative behaviour became an irritant to the court and he was ordered to limit his communications to his own defence counsel and to issues pertaining to his own defence... Goering wanted the German leaders in the dock to present a united front, an aim in which he could not succeed. The disparity among the defendants in their backgrounds and in their roles in relation to Hitler was too great... Goering's personal vanity was evident throughout the trial. When testimony was presented about his penchant for luxury or his looting of art works from occupied countries, he became visibly angry – more so than when the larger issues of his involvement with aggressive war and war crimes were the subject during his examination on the stand.'

Goering's Grandstanding

Jackson began his cross-examination.

'I want to get what's necessary to run the kind of a system that you set up in Germany and concentration camps was one of the things you found immediately necessary upon coming to power, was it not? And you set them up as a matter of necessity as you saw it?'

Goering remained calm and self-assured. He would not be led. He took every opportunity to deliver a self-serving sermon, in order to steer the argument away from the question of conspiracy to the complexities of administration.

'You asked me if I considered it necessary to establish concentration camps immediately in order to eliminate opposition. That is correct.'

To Jackson's chagrin the witness was permitted to make long convoluted speeches in an attempt to justify his actions, but every time Jackson made an attempt to curtail him he was overruled. There seemed to be no way of forcing him to answer the question, which was extremely frustrating for the American. By the end of that day it was perceived that Goering had won the first round. There were those among the press and the prosecution who hated all that Goering stood for, but who nevertheless admired his personal courage. He took full responsibility for the orders he had issued and then declared that he had no intention of 'hiding behind the Führer'.

As Major Neave later admitted, 'Murderer he may have been but he was a brave bastard too.'

On the second day, Goering spoke for almost five hours. After holding the court in rapt attention as he took the charges in the indictment to pieces one by one, he ended by declaring that the Führer principle – a hierarchy of leaders led by a supreme leader, who answered to no one – was not unique to the Nazi state. It was inspired by the papal hierarchy of the Catholic Church and the presidential system that had been adopted by the Soviet Union and the United States.

On the third day Goering concluded a total of 12 hours of testimony by quoting Winston Churchill who had stated, 'In a struggle for life and death there is no legality'. There was no denying that the fat man was ahead on points. It would take a skilled advocate to get him on the ropes.

Goering vs. Jackson

By the time Goering took the witness stand for the fourth day he was, as one observer remarked, 'fit, focused, lucid and fiercely unapologetic'. Jackson knew he faced a formidable adversary.

The larger-than-life figure had dominated the crowded courtroom in Nuremberg, the city that had once been the spiritual home of National Socialism and the site of the annual mass rallies. His wolfish grin and thin veneer of oily charm betrayed the relish with which he had seized the opportunity to strut once more on the world's stage. It was Goering who commanded the attention of the world's press, pens poised over their notebooks to witness the final act in the 'trial of the century'. By contrast, his co-defendants sat slumped in the dock like broken men in their shabby, ill-fitting civilian suits and uniforms shamefully stripped of badges of rank.

Even in captivity, Goering's fellow prisoners remained in his thrall, their fragile morale bolstered by his overbearing personality. If it had not been for Goering, Speer might have been able to persuade the more impressionable defendants to accept their share of responsibility for the atrocities perpetrated in the name of the Third Reich. The Führer was dead, the Reich was in ruins and Goering was now deprived of his

US prosecutor Robert H. Jackson (left) and Soviet assistant prosecutor General Uri Pokrovsky (right) listen intently during the summing-up.

medals and his comic operetta uniforms. However, he refused to see himself as a war criminal. He still played the role of the soldier and statesman who was determined to secure his place in history. Such conceit, combined with his refusal to acknowledge his complicity in these crimes, would be hard to crack.

Chief Justice Jackson began his questioning of the defendant in a quiet, measured tone, like a boxer intent on getting the measure of his opponent.

'Did you regard the elimination of the Jews from economic life as your responsibility?'

Goering assented, adding that he saw it as his duty to remove all Jewish industrialists from office, especially those in the armaments industry.

'Was that the first of your legal measures against the Jews?' Jackson inquired.

'I believe their removal from official posts was first, in 1933.'

The American was evidently attempting a new strategy, but what exactly that might be eluded Goering for the moment.

'And in 1936 you personally drafted an act making it punishable by death to transfer money abroad?'

It was clear now that Jackson sought only confirmation of his accusations as he brandished the damning document for all to see.

'That is correct.'

'And that Jews must pay for the damage caused by anti-Jewish riots with their insurance claims forfeited by the Reich?'

'I did sign a similar law but whether it is the same...'

Jackson cut him short.

'Did you not say about those riots, "I wish you had killed 200 Jews instead of destroying such valuables"?'

In a move calculated to intimidate, Jackson approached the witness stand and deposited the transcript of the conversation on the table, as if challenging the defendant to deny its very existence.

'But that was said in a moment of bad temper and extreme excitement.'

'Spontaneous sincerity, in other words,' Jackson observed.

Goering blanched.

Goering Signs His Own Death Warrant

'Did you not also sign a decree in 1940 ordering the seizure of all Jewish property in Poland?'

'I assume so if the decree is there.' The defendant was now visibly squirming in his seat.

'And another saying the Jews would receive no compensation for damage caused by enemy attack or by German forces?'

'If the law bears my name then it must be so,' Goering conceded.

'Is this your signature?' asked Jackson, pointing an accusing finger at the next document that had been laid before the accused.

'It appears to be.'

'Is it or is it not your signature?' Jackson's tone betrayed his growing impatience.

Goering sensed that a trap was being set. He took a moment to answer.

'It is.'

'It is your signature on a document dated July 1941,' Jackson explained for the benefit of the court, 'asking Himmler and [Reinhard] Heydrich to make plans for the Final Solution of the Jewish Question.'

Goering exploded.

'That is not a proper translation! I said total solution, not final solution.'

'These are your words to Himmler,' continued Jackson, warming to the task. '"I charge you to send me before long an overall plan for the organizational, factual and material measures necessary for the desired solution of the Jewish question." Is that an accurate translation of this order?'

'That had to do with the evacuation and emigration of the Jews,' Goering protested.

'You ordered all government agencies to co-operate with the SS in the final solution of the Jewish question. Did you not?'

'There is nothing in there about the SS!' The colour was coming back to Reichsmarschall Goering's flaccid cheeks.

'This document states that you ordered all government agencies to co-operate with the SS. You sent this letter to SS Gruppenführer Heydrich.'

'That does not mean that the SS had anything to do with the solution of the Jewish question!'

The words were barely out of his mouth when Goering realized that he had placed the noose around his own neck. There was an audible murmur in the court as Jackson leaned in to face his most formidable adversary.

'Would you mind repeating that?' he asked calmly.

'I must say this clearly. I did not know anything about what took place in the concentration camps or the methods used there. These things were kept secret from me.'

But Jackson was already striding back to the bench where his colleagues sat, jubilant in the knowledge that the murderous nature of the Nazi leadership had finally been exposed for all to see.

'I might add that even the Führer did not know the extent of what was happening.' Goering was rambling, desperate. But no one was listening.

Jackson spun on his heel and flipped open another file. He studied it for some seconds before addressing the defendant in a noticeably dismissive tone.

'Witness – before this court there is evidence that nearly 10 million people have been exterminated, murdered in cold blood. You mean to say that you did not know and Hitler did not know what took place in the camps?'

'Yes.'

Goering looked nervously around him. But the awkward, self-conscious smiles of those who had recently been seduced by his charm had been replaced by grim expressions set in stone. Even his fellow defendants were now averting their gaze in embarrassment or shame. The game was up. It was time for the truth.

'Did you know that Hitler said in 1943 in a recorded meeting with the Reich's Minister of Foreign Affairs [Ribbentrop] that "Jews should be exterminated or taken to concentration camps. There is no other possibility."'

As he said this, Jackson pointed to the white-haired defendant in the dock as if to remind him that Ribbentrop himself could be called to corroborate the accusation.

'The Minister of Foreign Affairs, Ribbentrop, talked with Hitler of extermination. You were above Ribbentrop. You were Hitler's second-in-command. You were in charge of the four-year economic plan so you knew all about the gold teeth and eyeglasses that the victims left behind. And you have heard that it took five minutes more to kill the women because they had to cut off their hair to make mattresses. And nothing was told to you about the material that came to you from these people that had been murdered?'

'No! No!' spat Goering. 'How can you imagine such a thing? I was laying down the outlines of the German economy.'

'The witness is excused.'

Jackson announced that he was done and then he strode back to the bench. No one had ever turned their back on Reichsmarschall Goering before.

'I am not finished,' Goering protested, unaccustomed to being cut short.

'The witness is excused,' repeated Judge Shawcross.

'But I am not finished,' Goering exclaimed.

The Judge raised his gavel. The session was adjourned.

Whitney Harris recalled the moment.

'When we got Goering into the matter of the specific crimes that he committed such as the persecution of the Jews, well, then he collapsed. He was a done witness, I'll tell you, because we had him so devastated on the Jewish issue that he had nothing to say.'

Massacre

Public perception of Goering's downfall was influenced by the press, who presented Jackson as the wily advocate who had boxed the Nazi leader into a corner before delivering the knockout blow. The truth was somewhat less dramatic and edifying. Jackson was an able advocate, but he was not strong on cross-examination. He preferred to build a case against the accused piece by piece until they were forced to face the facts that had condemned them. During the course of Goering's marathon cross-examination, Jackson had become flustered. Allowing his emotions to get the better of him, he had flung off his headphones in frustration.

Jackson blamed Lawrence for allowing Goering to use the witness box as a political platform – the prisoner had been able to make long-winded speeches without interruption. The judge was not alone in feeling that he was having to go into battle with one hand tied behind his back. Biddle confided in private that Lawrence was far too lenient. He felt sorry for Jackson as he watched him struggling to retain his authority against the undisputed heavyweight in the witness box. At one point Jackson appeared to lose his line of questioning altogether and he was humiliated when Goering offered to help him. But he recovered and his patience ultimately paid off.

But it was not a single-handed success. Part of the credit for unmasking the sneering hoodlum behind the medals must be given to Maxwell-Fyfe, whose masterful questioning of Goering had the accused looking frightened from the first. Maxwell-Fyfe was probing the shameful matter of the murder of 50 RAF officers, who had been recaptured after the 'Great Escape'. As commander-in-chief of the Luftwaffe, Goering was responsible for its prisoner of war camps, so he could have countermanded the so-called Sagan Order. This instructed German personnel to execute the prisoners in batches over several days and then cremate the bodies in an effort to destroy the evidence.

'I am suggesting to you that it is absolutely impossible and untrue that in these circumstances you knew nothing about it,' Sir David insisted. 'I am suggesting that

Sir David Maxwell-Fyfe (centre), British deputy chief prosecutor, leaving the courtroom. His unrelenting cross-examination of Hermann Goering is one of the most celebrated in legal history.

when every one of these officers of yours knew about it, you knew about it too and that you did nothing to prevent these men from being shot.'

Goering's defence was that he had not been present at the crucial meeting at which Hitler had issued the order, but Maxwell-Fyfe did not allow him to be vague on this point. He pressed him as he would have done any common criminal who had been under cross-examination at the Old Bailey. Finally, Goering became flustered and admitted that he might have been present after all. If so, he would have known of the Führer's order to have the recaptured prisoners of war shot.

By the end of the session Goering was enraged – his red face was twisted into a grimace that betrayed his true character. The genial statesman had been exposed as nothing more than Hitler's henchman.

Assassination Attempt

Hermann Goering might never have taken the witness stand had it not been for a vigilant sentry at the courthouse. As the trial entered its most dramatic phase, with witnesses called to recall their ordeal in the camps, United States Army sergeant Clancy Sigal loaded his 45 mm automatic and left his unit. His destination was Nuremberg. He told no one where he was going, or what was burning in his mind, because his mission was to assassinate Hermann Goering, the man he held personally responsible for the murder of millions of his race. Clancy was the only Jew in his unit, so he felt that he was responsible for exacting the only form of justice that was due to such a monster. He told NPR News how he felt.

'I wanted to look Hermann Goering in the eye and shoot him dead.'

But in the foyer of the Palace of Justice, the military policemen on guard refused to allow him to enter without checking in his weapon.

'At first I was angry. I'd stored up a lot of hatred for the top Nazis like Goering who'd operated the "Final Solution" to kill Jews. But inside the courtroom I felt something like relief. Suddenly, it was unthinkable to add one more act of violence to the solemn, businesslike presentation of evidence. Evidence which included the shrunken heads of tortured prisoners and lampshades made of human skin. It moved me beyond tears to a sort of numbness... For three days, I couldn't take my eyes off Goering, who lounged in the dock like a bored Roman emperor... As concentration camp survivors testified, I sometimes caught Goering's cold, unblinking stare, which was full of contempt for the Tribunal and the witnesses. When the prosecution showed films of piled-up corpses at Auschwitz, Goering kept turning his head away, sometimes in my direction. I'm ashamed to say he stared me down, because I'd never before felt myself in the presence of such unmitigated evil.'

Clancy returned to his unit without seeing Goering testify, but he followed the proceedings in the newspapers and on the radio and was dismayed to hear reporters speak of Goering's 'brazen lack of repentance' when cross-examined.

'Today, in the midst of a national debate on how to treat captured terror suspects, my mind flashes back to Room 600 at Furtherstrasse 22. We gave Goering and the other war criminals a chance not only to defend themselves, but in some cases, preach hate and violence. In a ruined Germany, where so many corpses still lay buried in the rubble, and life seemed so very fragile, we found it in ourselves to give the worst of men due process.'

Hoess – Commandant of Auschwitz

Dr Kurt Kauffmann, counsel for Ernst Kaltenbrunner, had an uphill struggle trying to convince the court that his client was unaware of conditions in the concentration camps and that he was not personally responsible for the slave labour programme. Then on Monday 15 April 1946 Kauffmann made a desperate and bizarre attempt to prove his point. He called Rudolf Hoess, the former commandant of Auschwitz, to testify on Kaltenbrunner's behalf. Hoess dutifully confirmed that Kaltenbrunner had never visited Auschwitz, but his affidavit revealed such a stunning disregard for human suffering that it damned Kaltenbrunner by association.

Asked about his clinical efficiency in disposing of thousands of human beings every day, Hoess responded blankly:

'Don't you see, we SS men were not supposed to think about these things; it never even occurred to us. And besides, it was something already taken for granted that the Jews were to blame for everything… It was not just newspapers like *Stürmer* but it was everything we ever heard. Even our military and ideological training took for granted that we had to protect Germany from the Jews.

'… We were all so trained to obey orders without even thinking that the thought of disobeying an order would never have occurred to anybody.'

It is a curious fact that certain members of Hitler's tyrannical regime were willing to testify against their former superiors, even in the knowledge that in so doing they would be incriminating themselves. Some had resigned themselves to their fate, while others may have entertained the hope that their co-operation might weigh in their favour. Surely no such thoughts were entertained by Hoess, who presumably agreed to testify in order to ensure his place in the history books as one of the most evil men who ever lived.

Rudolf Hoess boasted that he ran 'the greatest extermination centre of all time'.

His affidavit reveals what one historian called the 'banality of evil' and it supports the belief that the local population knew what was taking place in the camps, despite their repeated denials.

The Business of Extermination

Hoess confirmed the fact that hundreds of thousands of human beings had been killed at Auschwitz during the time he had been camp commandant. He could only estimate their number, he said, because he had been forbidden to keep a written record. It was SS Obersturmführer Adolf Eichmann who had organized the transportation and extermination of the inmates and who had boasted that a total of 2 million people had been murdered at the camp. Conveniently for Hoess, and the other defendants who used him to deflect attention from their own crimes, Eichmann had fled to South America in the closing weeks of the war and could not be called to the stand.

Hoess continued with his testimony:

'In the summer of 1941 I was summoned to Berlin to Reichsführer-SS Himmler to receive personal orders. He told me something to the effect – I do not remember the exact words – that the Führer had given the order for a final solution of the Jewish question. We, the SS, must carry out that order. If it is not carried out now then the Jews will later on destroy the German people. He had chosen Auschwitz on account of its easy access by rail and also because the extensive site offered space for measures ensuring isolation... He told me that I was not even allowed to say anything about it to my immediate superior Gruppenführer Glücks. This conference concerned the two of us only and I was to observe the strictest secrecy.'

Glücks, who was subordinate to Himmler, was the inspector of concentration camps at that time. Dr Kauffmann continued by asking Hoess to describe the measures taken to ensure that the location of the extermination compound at Birkenau was kept secret and that access to the site was strictly limited to the SS and civilians issued with special passes.

Hoess told the court that all new inmates who had been designated for death were ordered to strip naked before being marched off to the gas chamber. They would not have been aware of their fate, however, because certain precautions had been taken to deceive them. Kauffmann asked Hoess, a family man, if he had ever felt pity for the victims, who included women and children. He claimed that he had felt compassion for them, but that he had been acting under orders from Himmler. On one occasion, in 1942, Himmler personally inspected the camp and watched one such 'processing' from beginning to end. Eichmann was a more regular visitor.

Hoess then made a pathetic attempt to excuse the ill-treatment and the torture by

The boots of Jewish victims on display at the Auschwitz-Birkenau Museum. The Nazis conducted the genocide and subsequent processing of their victims' bodies and belongings on an industrial scale.

claiming that it had all been the work of 'over-zealous guards', who had been punished for their brutality. When he was asked about the 'shameful conditions' that existed when the Allied armies liberated the camps, he responded that it was all due to the destruction of the railway network and the Allied bombing.

> 'The number of the sick became immense. There were next to no medical supplies; epidemics raged everywhere. Internees who were capable of work were used over and over again. By order of the Reichsführer, even half-sick people had to be used wherever possible in industry. As a result every bit of space in the concentration camps which could possibly be used for lodging was overcrowded with sick and dying prisoners.'

The court listened with incredulity as Hoess claimed that he had never personally observed any instances of the ill-treatment of prisoners, but if any wrongdoing had taken place it would have been the fault of the guards who had been recruited from the occupied territories.

Before he concluded his questioning, Dr Kauffmann asked Hoess if the defendant Ernst Kaltenbrunner had signed the orders for executions at the camp. Hoess answered in the affirmative. Kaltenbrunner had been damned by his own official.

A Damning Affidavit

After a short recess, Colonel Jakob Amen was permitted to read into the record an affidavit dictated by Hoess on 5 April (Doc. 3868PS, vol. 33, 27579) which the witness confirmed had been given voluntarily and was true in all respects. It was one of the most cold-blooded confessions ever read in a court of law.

> 'I have been constantly associated with the administration of concentration camps since 1934, serving at Dachau until 1938; then as Adjutant in Sachsenhausen from 1938 to 1 May 1940, when I was appointed Commandant of Auschwitz. I commanded Auschwitz until 1 December 1943, and estimate that at least 2,500,000 victims were executed and exterminated there by gassing and burning, and at least another half million succumbed to starvation and disease making a total dead of about 3,000,000. This figure represents about 70 or 80 per cent of all persons sent to Auschwitz as prisoners, the remainder having been selected and used for slave labour in the concentration camp industries; included among the executed and burned were approximately 20,000 Russian prisoners of war (previously screened out of prisoner-of-war cages by the Gestapo) who were delivered at Auschwitz in Wehrmacht transports operated by regular Wehrmacht officers and men. The remainder of the total number of victims included about 100,000 German Jews, and great

numbers of citizens, mostly Jewish, from Holland, France, Belgium, Poland, Hungary, Czechoslovakia, Greece, or other countries. We executed about 400,000 Hungarian Jews alone at Auschwitz in the summer of 1944.

'Mass executions by gassing commenced during the summer of 1941 and continued until fall 1944. I personally supervised executions at Auschwitz until first of December 1943 and know by reason of my continued duties in the Inspectorate of Concentration Camps, WVHA, that these mass executions continued as stated above. All mass executions by gassing took place under the direct order, supervision, and responsibility of RSHA. I received all orders for carrying out these mass executions directly from RSHA.

'The "final solution" of the Jewish question meant the complete extermination of all Jews in Europe. I was ordered to establish extermination facilities at Auschwitz in June 1941. At that time, there were already in the General Government three other extermination camps: Belzek, Treblinka, and Wolzek. These camps were under the *Einsatzkommando* of the Security Police and SD. I visited Treblinka to find out how they carried out their exterminations. The camp commandant at Treblinka told me that he had liquidated 80,000 in the course of one-half year. He was principally concerned with liquidating all the Jews from the Warsaw Ghetto.

He used monoxide gas, and I did not think that his methods were very efficient. So when I set up the extermination building at Auschwitz, I used Zyklon B, which was a crystallized prussic acid which we dropped into the death chamber from a small opening. It took from three to 15 minutes to kill the people in the death chamber, depending upon climatic conditions. We knew when the people were dead because their screaming stopped. We usually waited about one-half hour before we opened the doors and removed the bodies. After the bodies were removed our special Kommandos took off the rings and extracted the gold from the teeth of the corpses.'

A can of Zyklon B gas from Mauthausen presented as evidence at the trial.

The terrible interior of one of the gas chambers at Auschwitz. Prisoners considered too weak to work were sent to the gas chamber; they were told they would be taking a shower. This chamber is preserved as part of the memorial to the Holocaust.

'All of the People... Knew'

Colonel Amen asked the witness to confirm under oath that what he had just read was all true and correct. Hoess answered that it was. Colonel Amen then asked what had been done with the gold which had been taken from the teeth of the corpses. Hoess answered that it had been melted down and shipped to the chief medical office of the SS in Berlin.

Colonel Amen resumed reading from the affidavit:

'Another improvement we made over Treblinka was that we built our gas chamber to accommodate 2,000 people at one time whereas at Treblinka their 10 gas chambers only accommodated 200 people each. The way we selected our victims was as follows: We had two SS doctors on duty at Auschwitz to examine the incoming transports of prisoners. The prisoners would be marched by one of the doctors who would make spot decisions as they walked by. Those who were fit for work were sent into the camp. Others were sent immediately to the extermination plants. Children of tender years were invariably exterminated since by reason of their youth they were unable to work. Still another improvement we made over Treblinka was that at Treblinka the victims almost always knew that they were to be exterminated and at Auschwitz we endeavoured to fool the victims into thinking that they were to go through a delousing process. Of course, frequently they realized our true intentions and we sometimes had riots and difficulties due to that fact. Very frequently women would hide their children under their clothes, but of course when we found them we would send the children in to be exterminated. We were required to carry out these exterminations in secrecy but of course the foul and nauseating stench from the continuous burning of bodies permeated the entire area and all of the people living in the surrounding communities knew that exterminations were going on at Auschwitz.'

Colonel Amen ending by asking the witness to confirm that what he had just read was true and correct.

Hoess answered that it was all true.

Inhabitants of the Warsaw ghetto are marched to an assembly point for transportation to Auschwitz.

A Moment of Truth

D r Goldensohn's diary entry for 9 April recorded a conversation that had taken place earlier that day with Goering, who had asked him how it was technically possible to murder two and a half million people at Auschwitz. Dr Goldensohn assured him that it was possible and he explained the practicalities in the same matter-of-fact manner that Hoess had adopted when he had confessed to him that morning. Each of the gas chambers could take up to 2,000 people at a time. It was the disposal of the bodies that slowed the ghastly process.

Dr Goldensohn noticed that Goering felt 'extremely uncomfortable' when he realized that Hoess' admission meant that the defendants could no longer deny the extent of the mass murders on the basis of the numbers alone. He had hoped, presumably, that the sheer number of people murdered in the camps would be too incredible for the court to believe. But Hoess had put paid to that. Goering sat lost in thought for a moment and then he asked how the order had been given. Goldensohn told him that Hoess had received it from Himmler himself, who had said that it was a direct order from the Führer.

'... that has nothing to do with loyalty,' Goering remarked in response to Dr Goldensohn's assertion that this was another example of blind loyalty, 'he could just as easily have asked for some other job – or something... Of course, somebody else would have done it anyway.'

When Goldensohn raised the possibility of assassinating Hitler, Goering snapped back at him.

'Oh, that is easily said, but you cannot do that sort of thing. What kind of a system would that be if anybody could kill the commanding officer if he didn't like his orders? You have got to have obedience in a military system.'

Goldensohn mused that millions of Germans were by now sick of their leaders' unquestioning obedience and he suggested that Goering should read an article in the *Nürnberger Nachrichten*, which bore the headline 'Blind Obedience without Conscience'.

'Ach, what the American-controlled newspapers print now does not mean a damn,' sneered the Reichsmarschall.

But Goldensohn noted that he 'seemed disturbed' at the thought that this was what the German people were reading and agreeing with while he and his fellow defendants were still trying to justify the Führer principle.

Conversations with Dr Gilbert

r Gilbert found Ribbentrop equally
unnerved by Hoess' shattering
confession.

'... Tell me,' said Ribbentrop, 'I wasn't
in court on Monday. Did Hoess actually
say that Hitler had ordered the mass
murders?'

Gilbert answered that Himmler had
given him a direct *Führerbefehl* for the
extermination of the Jews in 1941.

Ribbentrop held his head in his hands
and repeated the year like a mantra.

'My God! Did Hoess say in '41?... All
those years – a man to whom children
came so trustingly and lovingly. It must
have been a fanatic madness – there is no
doubt now that Hitler ordered it?
I thought even up to now that perhaps Himmler, late in the war, under some pretext...
But '41, he said? My God! My God!'

Dr Gilbert talks with some of the defendants during a recess in the proceedings.

During the Easter recess Dr Gilbert found some of the defendants in more reflective
mood. They seemed increasingly willing to share their thoughts. On the evening of
18 April, Goering looked dejected, but he was still on the defensive.

'Why, of course, the people don't want war,' he told Gilbert. 'Why would some
poor slob on a farm want to risk his life in a war when the best that he can get out of
it is to come back to his farm in one piece. Naturally, the common people don't want
war; neither in Russia, nor in England, nor in America, nor for that matter in Germany.
That is understood. But, after all, it is the leaders of the country who determine the
policy and it is always a simple matter to drag the people along, whether it is a
democracy, or a fascist dictatorship, or a parliament, or a communist dictatorship.'

Gilbert disagreed.

'In a democracy the people have some say in the matter through their elected
representatives, and in the United States only Congress can declare wars.'

But Goering was warming to his subject and would not be persuaded.

'Voice or no voice, the people can always be brought to the bidding of the leaders.
That is easy. All you have to do is tell them they are being attacked, and denounce the
pacifists for lack of patriotism and exposing the country to danger. It works the same
in any country.'

Empty Slogans

Goering was in the habit of giving spontaneous speeches whenever it seemed that morale among the defendants might be flagging. On one such occasion he turned his wrath upon Jodl, who had questioned Hitler's decision to commit suicide, leaving his acolytes to face their fate. He roared that it was tantamount to treason to think that it might have been better if the Führer had lived to be humiliated in court.

In a quiet moment later that day, Dr Gilbert asked Speer to explain Goering's capacity to dominate and intimidate the other defendants when he did not have a shred of real authority. Speer said there was something in the German character that responded instinctively to authority, real or imagined. However, he dismissed the assumption that Goering had expressed any significant ideas or thoughts. His words had been merely empty platitudes and slogans, he said, the very same banalities that had brought the party to power. Even the well-educated had fallen for these appeals to vanity and national pride, because they had enabled everyone to project their own hopes and fears on to the leadership. Such generalizations allowed everyone to hear whatever they wanted to hear.

Schacht Testifies

The other defendants made less dramatic appearances on the witness stand than Goering, but each of them revealed yet another facet of human frailty, an endless capacity for self-deception and the instinct to survive at all costs.

On 1 May Hjalmar Schacht sat impatiently in the witness box as Justice Jackson rifled through his papers in preparation for his cross-examination. The look on the banker's face might have struck terror into the hearts of his lowly clerks, but his imperious disdain made no impression on the chief justice. He rounded on Schacht and asked him to explain what he had meant when he said he had 'led rather than misled Hitler' on several occasions. Schacht muttered that he could attribute many successes to not having told his colleagues the truth, an admission for which Jackson thanked him. From that moment onwards, nothing that Schacht said on the stand could be assumed to be the truth.

Schacht continued by asserting that he had remained in office under the dictatorship to ensure the restoration of the German economy and 'international equality by means of armaments'. He denied that he had helped to bring Hitler to power, but he could not deny the fact that he had signed a petition drawn up by the

Hjalmar Schacht (standing, centre right) delivers his final statement to the court.

major industrialists, urging President Hindenburg to appoint Hitler as chancellor in 1933. When the banker declared that he had accepted a place in Hitler's cabinet so that he could work against the leadership from within, his words rang as hollow as his grating voice.

'Was it customary in Germany for a member of a government to attempt to defeat the leader?' Jackson asked.

Schacht retorted that it was not his intention to defeat the administration but to slow it down. He was a wily and obdurate man who was clearly not going to crack under cross-examination. His indefatigable self-belief had rendered him impervious to criticism, but his tacit endorsement of the regime and his repeated cry that he was only a banker would not be allowed to go unchallenged.

Before he left the witness stand on the second day of his cross-examination he shouted out to the court.

'I would have killed Hitler myself!'

But it was an unconvincing and melodramatic exit by a man whose admiration for Hitler had been revealed only hours earlier. A film had been shown of the Führer's triumphal return to Berlin after the fall of France in May 1940. Hitler was being greeted by cheering ecstatic crowds while his chief financier trotted dutifully beside him like a favourite pet. He was shaking his master's hand vigorously, patently eager to hold on for as long as possible.

Later that evening Justice Birkett confided in his diary that while Goering was taking a 'savage delight' in Schacht's discomfort, others on the bench were disappointed with Jackson's performance.

His low-key approach was not likely to lead to any of the accused blurting out something that might incriminate them or contradict their previous statements. What was needed was the cut and thrust of rapid question and answer, which would not give the witnesses time to think. They might then respond instinctively – and maybe even truthfully.

Hans Frank

The former governor-general of Poland had handed over 43 volumes of private diaries to the Americans in the hope that he would be seen as a mere functionary of the administration. But he was to be sorely disillusioned.

Frank's counsel, Dr Alfred Seidl, asked him how much he knew about the genocide to which he had so enthusiastically contributed.

'I, myself, speaking from the depths of my feelings and having lived through the five months of this trial, want to say that now after I have gained full insight into all the horrible atrocities which have been committed, I am possessed by a deep sense of guilt,' Frank replied.

'Did you ever participate in the annihilation of the Jews?' Seidl continued.

'I say "yes," and the reason why I say "yes," is because, having lived through the five months of the trial, and particularly after having heard the testimony of the witness Hoess, my conscience does not allow me to throw the responsibility solely on these minor people. I myself never installed an extermination camp for Jews, or promoted the existence of such camps, but if Adolf Hitler personally has laid that dreadful responsibility on his people, then it is mine too, for we have fought against Jewry for years, and we have indulged in the most terrible utterances – my own diary bears witness against me. Therefore, it is no more than my duty to answer your question with "yes". A thousand years will pass and still this guilt of Germany will not have been erased.'

His only defence lay in his assertion that it was misleading to choose incriminating phrases out of context and that he had been intoxicated by the spirit of the time, 'a wild and stormy period filled with many passions and when a whole country is on fire and a life and death struggle is going on, such words may easily be used.'

The sunglasses kept on by Hans Frank after leaving the courtroom perhaps betray a dawning sense of guilt.

Wilhelm Keitel

When Keitel took the stand to answer questions posed by his counsel, Dr Otto Nelte, he admitted that he had executed orders that were in violation of the laws governing the conduct of war and international law. But he claimed that his actions were those of any dutiful German officer who had taken an oath to obey his leader.

'As a soldier I must say that the term "War of Aggression" as used here is meaningless as far as I am concerned... According to my own personal feelings, the concept "war of aggression" is a purely political concept and not a military one... I think I can summarize my views by saying that military officers should not have authority to decide this question and are not in a position to do so; and that these decisions are not the task of the soldier, but solely that of the statesman...'

'But you are not only a soldier,' Nelte went on, 'you are also an individual with a life of your own. When facts brought to your notice in your professional capacity seemed to reveal that a projected operation was unjust, did you not give it consideration?'

'I believe I can truthfully say,' Keitel replied, 'that throughout the whole of my military career I was brought up, so to speak, in the old traditional concept that we never discussed this question. Naturally one has one's own opinion and a life of one's own, but in the exercise of one's professional functions as a soldier and an officer, one has given this life away, yielded it up. Therefore, I could not say either at that time or later that I had misgivings about questions of a purely political discretion, for I took the stand that a soldier has the right to have confidence in his state leadership, and accordingly he is obliged to do his duty and to obey.'

In the line of duty. Wilhelm Keitel (between Hitler on his left and Goebbels on his right) at the State Opera, Berlin.

'Unusual' Bank Deposits

When Walther Funk, president of the Reichsbank, came to testify he was asked if he had accepted any 'unusual' deposits during the war. Funk answered that he did not know what the prosecution meant. He was then shown a number of photographs of gold spectacle frames, rings, watches, earrings and gold teeth, all of which had been sent by the SS to the bank from the concentration camps. The items had been found in huge quantities in the vaults.

Funk responded that many people deposited valuables and that the bank was not required to ask them how they had been acquired. This prompted a sarcastic response from the prosecutor.

'Prior to 1939 precisely how many of your customers deposited their teeth into your bank?'

Walther Funk giving testimony on his own behalf. He pleaded innocence when questioned about the teeth and other gold items taken from concentration-camp victims that were found deposited inside the Reichsbank's vaults.

A Sworn Statement

Not all of the witnesses at Nuremberg appeared in person. For various reasons some chose to submit their testimonies in the form of sworn statements, which were read into the record by a member of the prosecution. However, this did not make them any less valid or less disturbing.

The most moving account had perhaps been dictated by German construction manager Hermann Graebe, who had witnessed the mass execution of Ukranian Jews near the city of Dubno on 5 October 1942. His testimony was read aloud by Sir Hartley Shawcross on 27 July 1946, as part of the prosecution case against the SS.

'On the 5 October 1942, when I visited the building office at Dubno, my foreman Moennikes told me that in the vicinity of the site Jews from Dubno had been shot in three large pits, each about thirty metres long and three metres deep. About fifteen hundred persons had been killed daily. All were to be liquidated. As the shootings had taken place in his presence he was still very upset.'

Graebe decided to see for himself so he persuaded Moennikes to drive back to the site. There they saw truck-loads of frightened people being ordered to undress by an SS man carrying a whip. They were told to put their shoes in one pile and their clothes in a separate pile. Graebe estimated that the pile of shoes must have contained 800 to 1,000 pairs. None of the SS men seemed to mind that they were being watched by the construction workers. As Graebe and Moennikes approached the pit they heard a quick succession of shots from behind one of the earth mounds. Nearby, the next batch of victims was already being prepared for execution.

'Without screaming or weeping these people undressed, stood in family groups, kissed each other, said their farewells, and waited for a sign from another SS man, who stood near the pit, also with a whip in his hand.

'During the fifteen minutes that I stood near the pit, I did not hear anyone complain or beg for mercy. I watched a family of about eight, a man and a woman, both about fifty, with their children, aged about one, eight and ten, and two grown-up daughters of about twenty to twenty-four.

'An old woman with snow-white hair was holding the one-year-old child in her arms, singing something to it and tickling it. The child was crowing with delight. The man and wife were looking on with tears in their eyes.

'The father was holding the hand of a boy about ten, speaking to him softly. The boy was fighting back his tears. The father pointed to the sky, stroked the boy's head and seemed to explain something to him.'

Cold-Blooded Murder

At that moment the SS troops ordered the first 20 people to go behind the mound. When Graebe followed them he found himself standing before an enormous grave in which the victims lay so closely packed that only their heads were visible. Some of them were clearly still alive.

'The pit was already two-thirds full. I estimated that it already contained about one thousand people. I looked round for the man who had shot them. He was an SS man who was sitting on the edge of the narrow end of the pit, his legs dangling into it. He had a sub-machine gun across his knees and was smoking a cigarette.

'The people, completely naked, went down some steps which had been cut in the clay wall of the pit and climbed over the heads of those already lying there, to the place indicated by the SS man. They laid down in front of the dead or injured people. Some of them caressed those who were still alive and spoke to them softly.

'Then I heard a series of shots. I looked into the pit and saw that the bodies were twitching or that the heads lay motionless on top of the bodies which lay before them. Blood was pouring from their necks.

'I was surprised I was not ordered away, but saw there were also two or three uniformed policemen standing nearby. The next batch was already approaching. They climbed into the pit, lined up against the previous victims and were shot.'

Shortly afterwards Graebe witnessed the arrival of another truck, this time packed with the elderly and infirm. Those who were too frail to walk to the pit were undressed and carried by the others. Then the shooting resumed.

On the following day Graebe returned to the site with his workers. He saw about 30 naked people lying near the edge of the pit, some of whom were still alive and staring straight in front of them. Moments later an SS detail arrived. They ordered the survivors to throw the corpses into the pit and then follow them in, when they were shot dead.

The Case Against the German Army

The long-standing enmity between the SS and the Wehrmacht emerged during the tribunal's ongoing investigation into the last of the indicted organizations, the German General Staff and the High Command. Former members of the Waffen-SS and their defence counsel testified that the regular German army was to blame for many of the murderous acts of which they had been accused. But this crude and shameful tactic was exposed by Dr Hans Laternser, counsel for the German General Staff, who skilfully dismantled the accusations piece by piece. In this he was assisted by the testimony of Field Marshals von Rundstedt, von Manstein, List, von Leeb and Kesselring, who convinced the tribunal that they were credible witnesses.

American prosecutors (seated) listen to Dr Hans Laternser (standing, bottom left), legal counsel to the German General Staff and Oberkommando der Wehrmacht (OKW; High Command of the Armed Forces).

General Gerd von Rundstedt, a soldier for 54 years, listens attentively. Known by some of his troops as the 'Black Knight', he insisted that Hitler made military decisions without consulting his generals.

Dr Laternser argued that these senior officers did not form an identifiable group and so could not be condemned as a criminal organization – unlike the SS, which had been created as a unit and had recruited members who adhered to its ideals. Furthermore, the senior commanders of the Wehrmacht had not conspired to wage an aggressive war, but instead had trained the armed forces for the defence of Germany. It was the Nazi government that had decided to invade and subdue Europe, not the regular army, which now sought to distance itself from the regime. Dr Laternser argued vigorously and persuasively that Germany's military leaders had not conspired with the SS and the Gestapo to commit war crimes and that after 1941 it was not possible for them to resign without serious consequences for themselves and their families.

⚖️

The arid and aristocratic von Rundstedt claimed under oath that Hitler's reoccupation of the Rhineland in 1936 had come as a complete surprise and that he had heard about it first on the radio. This statement was greeted by derisive laughter in the court, but von Rundstedt was adamant.

'Hitler held conferences merely to inform his generals of his intentions,' he said.

The tribunal agreed that senior army officers had, in many cases, ignored orders to murder political opponents and civilians in the occupied countries and that they had sometimes avoided killing captured commandos, but they were not exonerated.

In summing up the prosecution case against the General Staff, Brigadier Telford Taylor declared that:

'... merely because some of the military leaders disapproved of the order, it was not executed as often as it otherwise might have been. But this defence is worse than worthless; it is shameful.'

The tribunal, however, reluctantly agreed with the defence in principle and ruled that the military leadership did not constitute a criminal organization. However, the commanders did not escape without criticism. The judgement found that:

'They have been a disgrace to the honourable profession of arms. Without their military guidance the aggressive ambitions of Hitler and his fellow Nazis would have been academic and sterile. Although they were not a group... they were certainly a ruthless military caste... Many of these men have made a mockery of the soldier's oath of obedience to military orders. When it suits their defence they say they had to obey: when confronted with Hitler's brutal crimes, which are shown to have been within their general knowledge, they say they disobeyed.'

Officers who were accused of war crimes, such as von Manstein, were later indicted as individuals and put on trial in Nuremberg and the other zones of occupation.

Job well done. David Maxwell-Fyfe (centre), one of the British prosecutors, leaves court on 30 September 1946 – verdict day.

The Hitler Gang

'Let the whole damn Nazi system and all who participated in it, including myself, go down with the ignominy and disgrace it deserves.'

ALBERT SPEER, IN CONVERSATION WITH DR GILBERT

In the corridors of the Palace of Justice, it was no secret that Goering and Speer hated and distrusted each other almost as much as they hated the other members of the Hitler gang. While Hitler was alive they were held in check by his domineering will, but now he was gone they were scrabbling at each other's throats in a desperate effort to save their own necks. Speer's strategy was brazen and bold – it was to ingratiate himself with the Allied prosecution by informing on his fellow defendants. By strengthening the prosecution case he hoped to increase his own chances of escaping the death penalty. He also told Dr Gilbert that Goering's intimidating presence was preventing some of his co-defendants from revealing their roles in the regime. Acting on this information, Colonel Andrus ordered that Goering was to eat alone in his cell from then on, while the others were to be isolated from each other at meal times.

Speer's actions made him the bitter enemy of Goering, who called Speer a traitor to his face.

'How could he stoop so low to save his lousy life?' Goering asked Dr Gilbert.

And when Speer declared that they were all 'corrupt cowards in the country's hour of crisis' and that Goering had planned to hand Himmler over to the Allies, Goering was furious.

'Do you think I would have handed over Himmler to the enemy? I would have liquidated the bastard myself.'

Albert Speer in consultation with his two defence attorneys in the defence-counsel conference room. He desperately tried to deny all knowledge of the terrible conditions in which slave labourers worked.

The Cross-Examination
of Albert Speer

Speer's good looks and urbane charm persuaded some of the more forgiving members of the court that his remorse was genuine and that he was in a different category to his fellow defendants – but he was also considered devious, cunning and manipulative. He would not be led into a trap as easily as Goering had been. A different approach would be needed to expose the full extent of Speer's responsibility for the slave workers who had been commandeered to toil to their deaths in the munitions factories.

Jackson opened with a stinging riposte to Speer's claim that he knew nothing of the conditions in the concentration camps.

'You have stated a good many of the matters for which you were not responsible, and I want to make clear just what your sphere of responsibility was. You were not only a member of the Nazi Party after 1932, but you held high rank in the Party, did you not?'

Speer confirmed this. He also admitted that in October 1942 he had recommended sending sick and slow workers from the factories under his control to concentration camps, in order to 'encourage' the others to be more productive.

'Let it happen several times,' he had said 'and the news will soon get around.'

Speer sought to defend his actions.

'It was one of the many remarks one can make in wartime when one is upset.'

Jackson then put it to the witness that it was common knowledge that the concentration camps were places where harsh treatment, to put it mildly, was meted out to the inmates.

'Yes, but not to the extent which has been revealed in this trial... I assert that a great number of the foreign workers in our country did their work quite voluntarily once they had come to Germany.'

Jackson looked visibly stunned at Speer's effrontery.

'Well, we will take that up later,' he said.

Asked if he was aware of his government's attitude to the Jews, Speer was again evasive. He stated in all seriousness that he had known that it was Nazi party policy to 'evacuate' all Jews from Germany.

Jackson then confronted Speer with a direct accusation.

'There is no question that they were put into labour corps or collected for removal, is there?'

Speer could not deny it.

'That is correct.'

Asked about his knowledge of the use of slave workers, Speer admitted that they were brought to Germany against their will and that he had voiced no objections. On the contrary, he confessed to having made a considerable effort to procure as many slave workers and Russian prisoners as possible for his armaments factories. He had done this in the full knowledge that using prisoners of war was strictly forbidden by the Geneva Convention.

After a recess, Jackson returned to the subject of slave workers and specifically Speer's knowledge of the conditions at the Krupp steel works at Essen, which he admitted to having visited on five or six occasions. According to Krupp's own records there were 39,245 foreign workers and 11,234 prisoners of war in their factories in 1943. Within a year that figure had increased to 54,990 foreign workers and 18,902 prisoners of war. Speer denied that he had any knowledge of the conditions under which these workers were kept, claiming that he was only concerned with productivity. That did not deter Justice Jackson from reading affidavits from German employees into the record, in which they described the starvation diet and other deprivations that were suffered by the Russian prisoners of war. Speer coldly dismissed it all as the result of Allied bombing.

Torture and Maltreatment

Speer could not, however, so readily dismiss the testimony (exhibit 894) of Herr Homer, a Krupp employee who described the torture and maltreatment of French, Italian and other foreign workers by Lowenkamp, an overseer. According to Homer's written statement

> 'He had a steel cabinet built which was so small that one could hardly stand in it. He locked up foreigners in the box, women too, for 48 hours at a time without giving the people food. They were not released even to relieve nature. It was forbidden for other people, too, to give any help to the persons locked in, or to release them. While clearing a concealed store he fired on escaping Russian civilians without hitting any of them.
>
> 'One day, while distributing food, I saw how he hit a French civilian in the face with a ladle and made his face bleed. Further, he delivered Russian girls without bothering about the children afterwards. There was never any milk for them so the Russians had to nourish the children with sugar water.'

Jackson broke off to say that this statement was only a small sample of a much larger amount of similar material, which he assumed the witness would also disregard as exaggerated. Speer's composure was beginning to crack. He damned the affidavit as a lie and denied that German civilians were capable of such acts.

'Well, what about the steel boxes?' asked Jackson. 'Was that also a lie?'

'Yes,' Speer said. 'That was another lie.'

The Labour Camp at Essen

Jackson then read from another sworn affidavit, Document 258 (USA 896), which established that the SS were being used as the guards at Essen. It had been made under oath before a military court by Hubert Karden.

> 'The camp inmates were mostly Jewish women and girls from Hungary and Romania. The camp inmates were brought to Essen at the beginning of 1944 and were put to work at Krupp's. The accommodation and feeding of the camp prisoners was beneath all dignity. At first the prisoners were accommodated in simple wooden huts. These huts were burned down during

an air raid and from that time on the prisoners had to sleep in a damp cellar. Their beds were made on the floor and consisted of a straw-filled sack and two blankets. In most cases it was not possible for the prisoners to wash themselves daily, as there was no water. There was no possibility of having a bath. I could often observe from the Krupp factory, during the lunch break, how the prisoners boiled their under-clothing in an old bucket or container over a wood fire, and cleaned themselves.'

In the event of an air-raid the female prisoners were left to seek shelter in a ditch while the SS troops ran to their underground concrete bunker. On a normal day, the women were woken at 5 am, after which they had to undergo a 45-minute march to the factory. They worked there until 6 pm with only a 30-minute break for food, which consisted of potato peelings. Many were malnourished as a result, but they still had to undertake hard physical labour. On the march back to the camp, the female guards routinely beat and abused them.

A view of the interior of the Krupps munitions works in Essen, Germany. The foreign workers and prisoners of war working here lived in appalling conditions and were abused by the SS.

Jackson turned on Speer.

'In your estimation that, I suppose, is also an exaggeration?'

After a short recess Speer returned to the stand and was presented with photographic evidence of the existence of torture devices installed at the Krupp works at Essen. Jackson read the descriptions aloud for the benefit of the court.

'Photograph "A" shows an iron cupboard which was specially manufactured by the firm of Krupp to torture Russian civilian workers to an extent that cannot possibly be described by words. Men and women were often locked into a compartment of the cupboard, in which hardly any man could stand up for long periods. The measurements of this compartment are: Height 1.52 metres; breadth and depth 40 to 50 centimetres each. Frequently even two people were kicked and pressed into one compartment... At the top of the cupboard there are a few sieve-like air holes through which cold water was poured on the unfortunate victims during the ice-cold winter.'

The Doctor's Story

Jackson announced that he had access to more than a hundred statements and depositions relating to the labour camp at Essen, but that he would not offer them into evidence because they were all of a similar nature. However, he felt it necessary to submit one more, Document 313 (Exhibit USA-901) in which a Polish army physician, Dr Apolinary Gotowicki, described the conditions endured by 1,800 Russian, Polish and French prisoners of war in the Krupp factories and the adjoining labour camp at Raumastrasse.

Chief Justice Jackson began to read:

'There was a big hall in the camp which could house about 200 men comfortably, in which 300 to 400 men were thrown together in such a catastrophic manner that no medical treatment was possible. The floor was cement and the mattresses on which the people slept were full of lice and bugs. Even on cold days the room was never heated and it seemed to me, as a doctor, unworthy of human beings that people should find themselves in such a position. It was impossible to keep the place clean because of the overcrowding of these men who had hardly room to move about normally. Every day at least 10 people were brought to me whose bodies were covered with bruises on account of the continual beatings with rubber tubes, steel switches, or sticks. The people were often writhing with agony and it was impossible for me to give them even a little medical aid. In spite of the fact that I protested, made complaints and petitions, it was impossible for me to protect the people or see that they got a day off from work.'

At great danger to himself, Dr Gotowicki approached the factory's directors and administrators to plead for better conditions and increased rations, but he was refused out of hand. In desperation he often gave his own meagre rations to the inmates. From 1941, despite his protests, conditions deteriorated.

> **'The food consisted of a watery soup which was dirty and sandy, and often the prisoners of war had to eat cabbage which was bad and stank. I could notice people daily who, on account of hunger or ill-treatment, were slowly dying. Dead people often lay for 2 or 3 days on the beds until their bodies stank so badly that fellow prisoners took them outside and buried them somewhere. The dishes out of which they ate were also used as toilets because they were too tired or too weak from hunger to get up and go outside. At 3 o'clock they were wakened. The same dishes were then used to wash in and later for eating out of. This matter was generally known. In spite of this it was impossible for me to get even elementary help or facilities in order to get rid of these epidemics, illnesses, or cases of starvation.'**

There was never any offer of medical aid or supplies. Doctor Gotowicki ended his deposition by describing the condition of the prisoners on their return to the camp each evening. Many collapsed on the march and had to be wheeled back in barrows or carried by their comrades. Accidents were frequent and of a serious nature, but Doctor Gotowicki was forbidden to prevent them from working, even for a single day. By 1942, three to four workers were dying daily.

Confronted with such testimony, Speer could only protest that the conditions were the result of wartime rationing and Allied bombing and that German workers also lived under 'difficult' conditions. The torture cabinets were merely clothes lockers and the prisoners were feigning illness because they had been told to do so by Allied propaganda leaflets! He spoke at length of administrative problems with such indifference that one might have mistaken him for a provincial council official discussing the local amenities. His only concession to the charges was to admit that he took responsibility for the policies that had resulted in the privations at slave labour camps such as those at Krupps, but that he could not be held accountable for specific 'excesses'.

Closing Speeches

The defence finally rested on 25 July 1946. On the following day the curtain rose on the final act of the 'trial of the century' as Chief Justice Jackson and the British prosecutor Sir Hartley Shawcross delivered their closing speeches. Jackson spoke at great length about the legal quagmire that the tribunal had been forced to navigate in its attempt to be fair and just to both sides. He concluded, as he had begun, with one of the most powerful and eloquent indictments of the nature of evil ever recorded.

Chief Justice Jackson, chief US prosecutor delivering his final summary. His historic speech still stands as one of the greatest indictments of human evil.

'It is impossible in summation to do more than outline with bold strokes the vitals of this Trial's mad and melancholy record... events which will live as the historical text of the twentieth century's shame and depravity.

'...We have presented to this Tribunal an affirmative case based on incriminating documents which are sufficient, if unexplained, to require a finding of guilt on Count One against each defendant. In the final analysis, the only question is whether the defendants' own testimony is to be credited against the documents and other evidence of their guilt. What, then, is their testimony worth? The fact is that the Nazi habit of economizing in the use of truth pulls the foundations out from under their own defences. Lying has always been a highly approved Nazi technique. Hitler, in *Mein Kampf*, advocated mendacity as a policy. Von Ribbentrop admits the use of the "diplomatic lie". Keitel advised that the facts of rearmament be kept secret so that they could be denied at Geneva (EC-177). Raeder deceived about rebuilding the German Navy in violation of Versailles. Goering urged Ribbentrop to tell a "legal lie" to the British Foreign Office about the *Anschluss*, and in so doing only marshalled him the way he was going (2947-PS). Goering gave his word of honour to the Czechs and proceeded to break it (TC-27). Even Speer proposed to deceive the French into revealing the specially trained among their prisoners (R-124). Nor is the lie direct the only means of falsehood. They all speak with a Nazi double talk with which to deceive the unwary. In the Nazi dictionary of sardonic euphemisms "final solution" of the Jewish problem was a phrase which meant extermination, "special treatment" of prisoners of war meant killing; "protective custody" meant concentration camp; "duty labour" meant slave labour; and an order to "take a firm attitude" or "take positive measures" meant to act with unrestrained savagery...

'When for years they have deceived the world, and masked falsehood with plausibility, can anyone be surprised that they continue their habits of a lifetime in this dock? Credibility is one of the main issues of this Trial. Only those who have failed to learn the bitter lessons of the last decade can doubt that men who have always played on the unsuspecting credulity of generous opponents would not hesitate to do the same, now. It is against such a background that these defendants now ask this Tribunal to say that they are not guilty of planning, executing, or conspiring to commit this long list of crimes and wrongs. They stand before the record of this Trial as bloodstained Gloucester stood by the body of his slain king. He begged of the widow, as they beg of you: "Say I slew them not." And the Queen replied, "Then say they were not slain. But dead they are..." If you were to say of these men that they are not guilty, it would be as true to say that there has been no war, there are no slain, there has been no crime.'

New Laws for Old Crimes

Jackson was followed by the British attorney-general Sir Hartley Shawcross. He closed the British prosecution case by clarifying the definition of aggressive war and reaffirming that under the Charter of the International Military Tribunal it was a crime to assist in the planning, preparation and initiation of a war which was in violation of international treaties.

There was no question of Hitler's invasion of Europe and Russia being a war of self-defence and military leaders such as Alfred Jodl and Wilhelm Keitel were not able to claim that there had been no law forbidding them from instigating such a war. An act that any reasonable person would consider to be wrong or injurious to the innocent can and should be condemned and punished, even if there is no existing law to enforce it. It was no defence for the first men accused of murder to complain that no court had heard such a case before. The Charter had not been drawn up to legitimize the prosecution of a defeated enemy, but to offer a means by which a number of injured nations could use existing laws to collectively prosecute those they considered had committed crimes on an unprecedented scale. If individuals invaded another state with the intention of committing robbery and murder, should they be allowed to shelter under the anonymity of the regime which they had helped to create, or should they answer for their individual acts of criminality?

'Some, it may be are more guilty than others; some played a more direct and active part than others in these frightful crimes. But when these crimes are such as you have to deal with here: slavery, mass murder and world war, when the consequences of the crimes are the deaths of over 20 million of our fellow men, the devastation of a continent, the spread of untold tragedy and suffering throughout the world, what mitigation is it that some took less part than others, that some were principals and others mere accessories. What matters if some forfeited their lives only a thousand times when others deserved a million deaths?... Liberty, love, understanding comes to this Court and cries: "These are our laws – let them prevail!" '

159

The Last Broadcast

On 31 August the court heard the defendants' closing pleas, joined by a worldwide audience listening in on the radio.

Albert Speer later wrote,

'They were the last chance to address our own people and also our last chance, by admitting our guilt, by facing squarely the crimes of the past to show the nation that we had led astray, a way out of its quandary.'

This wide-angle photograph was taken from the sound camera booth during the testimony of Colonel-General Alfred Jodl. It clearly shows the charged and intense atmosphere of the crowded courtroom, which had become the focus of world attention.

The stern, impassive countenance of Alfred Jodl, chief of operations for the German High Command (OKW), on the witness stand. He remains well groomed and his uniform is immaculately pressed.

He offered a faltering apology, although his sincerity is questionable:

'I should like to say something of fundamental importance here. This war has brought an inconceivable catastrophe upon the German people, and indeed, started a world catastrophe. Therefore, it is my unquestionable duty to assume my share of responsibility for this disaster before the German people. This is all the more my obligation, all the more my responsibility, since the head of the government has avoided responsibility before the German people, and before the world. I, as an important member of the leadership of the Reich, therefore, share in the total responsibility.'

Other defendants made a token gesture of contrition in mitigation, but few were convincing. The evidence had failed to uncover any serious effort on their part to counter or even condemn the orders they had so enthusiastically obeyed.

After Jodl's final plea, Justice Birkett could not refrain from commenting.

'I am always struck by the apparently sincere and passionate idealism of so many of these defendants – but what ideals!'

Walther Funk confessed to a sense of guilt, but he denied any personal wrongdoing.

> **'I said this morning that I had a deep sense of guilt and a deep sense of shame about the things which were done to the Jews in Germany, and that at the time when the terror and violence began I was involved in a strong conflict with my conscience. I felt, I could almost say, that a great injustice was being done. However, I did not feel guilty in respect to the Indictment against me here, that is, that according to the Indictment I was guilty of Crimes against Humanity because I signed the directives for carrying out laws which had been issued by superior officers – laws that had to be made so that the Jews would not be entirely deprived of their rights, and so that they would be given some legal protection at least in regard to compensation and settlement. I am admitting a guilt against myself, a moral guilt, but not a guilt because I signed the directives for carrying out the laws; in any event not a guilt against humanity.'**

Ribbentrop rallied to deliver an impassioned plea to the West, warning them of the dangers posed by the Soviet Union. Keitel, too, spoke with some dignity.

> **'I may have made many mistakes and perhaps I was weak, but of one thing you cannot accuse me – that I was cowardly, that I was dishonourable, or that I was faithless.'**

Hess rambled incoherently until Goering and Ribbentrop tried to stop him. He then snarled at them to 'shut up', at which point Lawrence intervened to silence him before the proceedings descended into farce. The final speeches of Rosenberg and Kaltenbrunner were equally unremarkable – Rosenberg's was vague and insubstantial and Kaltenbrunner's was a reiteration of his former denials. After ten intense and often tediously monotonous months in court even the indefatigable Goering was flagging at the finish. In his closing address the Reichsmarschall was no longer forceful, but he remained stubbornly unrepentant – he even reaffirmed his loyalty to his dead leader.

It was an anti-climactic end to a trial that had uncovered horrors that seemed simply too appalling to be true. It would take time for the enormity and the significance of what had taken place to be fully understood. The court was adjourned until 23 September in order to allow time for the judges to consider their verdicts.

The defendants in the dock. Joachim von Ribbentrop (standing), Germany's foreign minister from 1938 to 1945, delivers his final address to the court.

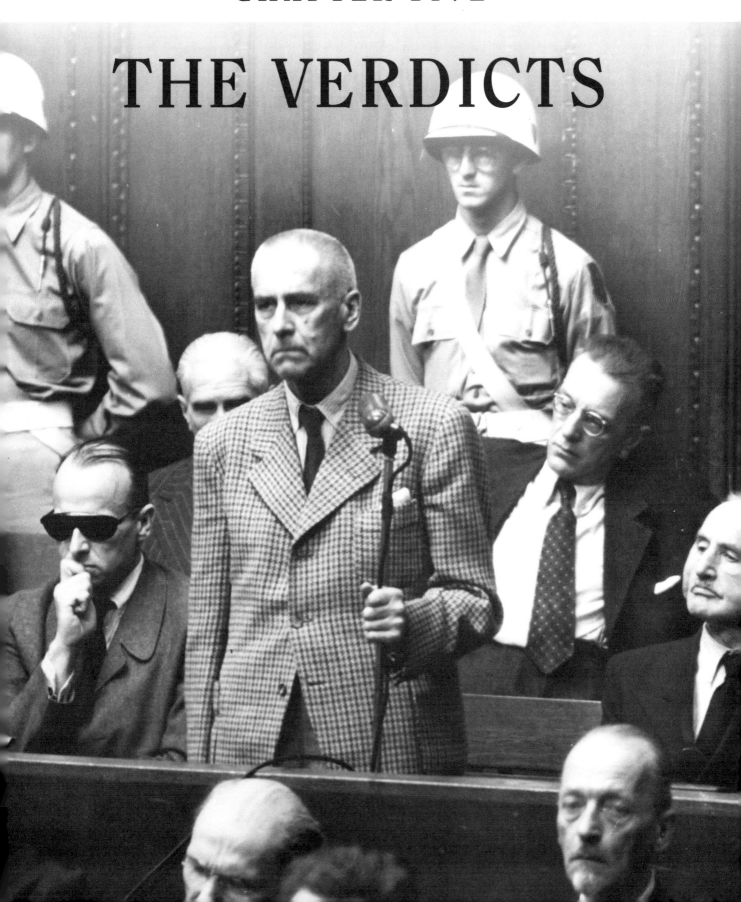

CHAPTER FIVE

THE VERDICTS

Lord Justice Lawrence (centre), the chief British judge and president of the tribunal, reads out part of the verdict which was delivered on 30 September and 1 October 1946. Each of the eight judges took turns in reading out the verdicts.

Those who seek to portray the leaders of the Third Reich as men misled by a madman, or who would depict the members of its criminal organizations, such as the SS, as honourable soldiers maligned by their enemies, would do well to study the judgments read to the defendants on 1 October 1946, the final day of the trial of the major Nazi war criminals at Nuremberg. Having considered the voluminous amount of evidence, both written and oral, some of it from their own people and all of it verified by official stamps and signatures, the judges arrived at the following verdicts.

Hermann Goering

VERDICT: Guilty on all 4 counts. Sentenced to death by hanging.

The Judgment against Goering concluded:

'From the moment he joined the Party in 1922 and took command of the street fighting organization, the SA, Goering was the adviser, the active agent of Hitler and one of the prime leaders of the Nazi movement. As Hitler's political deputy he was largely instrumental in bringing the National Socialists to power in 1933, and was charged with consolidating this power and expanding German armed might. He developed the Gestapo and created the first concentration camps, relinquishing them to Himmler in 1934... The night before the invasion of Czechoslovakia and the absorption of Bohemia and Moravia, at a conference with Hitler and President Hácha he threatened to bomb Prague if Hácha did not submit... He commanded the Luftwaffe in the attack on Poland and throughout the aggressive wars which followed... The record is filled with Goering's admissions of his complicity in the use of slave labour... He made plans for the exploitation of Soviet territory long before the war on the Soviet Union... Goering persecuted the Jews, particularly after the November, 1938, riots and not only in Germany... Although their extermination was in Himmler's hands, Goering was far from disinterested or inactive despite his protestations from the witness box... There is nothing to be said in mitigation... His guilt is unique in its enormity. The record discloses no excuses for this man.'

Hermann Goering in his corpulent heydey. Sentenced to death, his request to be shot, as befitted a soldier, rather than hanged as a common criminal, was denied.

Rudolf Hess

VERDICT: **Guilty on counts 1 and 2. Sentenced to life imprisonment.**

The Judgment against Hess concluded:

'… As deputy to the Führer, Hess was the top man in the Nazi Party with responsibility for handling all Party matters and authority to make decisions in Hitler's name on all questions of Party leadership… Hess was an informed and willing participant in German aggression against Austria, Czechoslovakia, and Poland… On September 27, 1938, at the time of the Munich crisis, he arranged with Keitel to carry out the instructions of Hitler to make the machinery of the Nazi Party available for a secret mobilization… With him on his flight to England, Hess carried certain peace proposals which he alleged Hitler was prepared to accept. It is significant to note that this flight took place only 10 days after the date on which Hitler fixed the time for attacking the Soviet Union… That Hess acts in an abnormal manner, suffers from loss of memory, and has mentally deteriorated during this trial, may be true. But there is nothing to show that he does not realize the nature of the charges against him, or is incapable of defending himself… There is no suggestion that Hess was not completely sane when the acts charged against him were committed.'

Joachim von Ribbentrop

VERDICT: **Guilty on all four counts. Sentenced to death by hanging.**

The Judgment against von Ribbentrop concluded:

'Ribbentrop was not present at the Hossbach Conference held on November 5, 1937 (at which Hitler revealed his war plans), but on January 2, 1938, while Ambassador to England, he sent a memorandum to Hitler indicating his opinion that a change in the status quo in the East in the German sense could only be carried out by force and suggesting methods to prevent England and France from intervening in a European war fought to bring about such a change… Ribbentrop participated in the aggressive plans against Czechoslovakia. Beginning in March 1938, he was in close touch with the Sudeten German Party and gave them instructions which had the effect of keeping the Sudeten German question a live issue which might serve as an excuse for the attack which Germany was planning against Czechoslovakia… After the Munich Pact he continued to bring diplomatic pressure with the object of occupying the remainder of Czechoslovakia… Ribbentrop played a

Neville Chamberlain (second from right), British prime minister from 1937 to 1940 and advocate of pre-war 'appeasement', walks alongside Ribbentrop (to his immediate right) on a visit to Germany in 1938. Adolf Hitler (on Ribbentrop's right) casts a penetrating glance left.

particularly significant role in the diplomatic activity which led up to the attack on Poland. He participated in a conference held on August 12, 1939, for the purpose of obtaining Italian support if the attack should lead to a general European war. Ribbentrop discussed the German demands with respect to Danzig and the Polish Corridor with the British Ambassador in the period from August 25 to August 30, 1939, when he knew that the German plans to attack Poland had merely been temporarily postponed in an attempt to induce the British to abandon their guarantee to the Poles... He played an important part in Hitler's "Final Solution" of the Jewish question. In September, 1942, he ordered the German diplomatic representatives accredited to various satellites to hasten the deportation of the Jews to the East... Ribbentrop participated in all the Nazi aggressions from the occupation of Austria to the invasion of the Soviet Union... It was because Hitler's policy and plans coincided with his own ideas that Ribbentrop served him so willingly to the end.'

Wilhelm Keitel

VERDICT: Guilty on all four counts. Sentenced to death by hanging.

The Judgment against Keitel concluded:

'... Keitel was present on May 23, 1939, when Hitler announced his decision "to attack Poland at the first suitable opportunity." Already he had signed the directive requiring the Wehrmacht to submit its "Fall Weiss" timetable (for the attack on Poland) to OKW (Oberkommando Der Wehrmacht – Armed Forces High Command) on May 1... Hitler had said, on May 23, 1939, that he would ignore the neutrality of Belgium and the Netherlands, and Keitel signed orders for the attacks on October 15, November 20, and November 28, 1939... Keitel testified that he opposed the invasion of the Soviet Union for military reasons, and also because it would constitute a violation of the Non-Aggression Pact. Nevertheless, he initiated "Case Barbarossa" (for the attack on Russia) signed by Hitler on December 18, 1940, and attended the OKW discussion with Hitler on February 3, 1941... On August 4, 1942, Keitel issued a directive that paratroopers were to be turned over to the SD. On September 16, 1941, Keitel ordered that attacks on soldiers in the East should be met by putting to death 50 to 100 Communists for one German soldier, with the comment that human life was less than nothing in the East... Superior orders, even to a soldier, cannot be considered in mitigation where crimes as shocking and extensive have been committed consciously, ruthlessly.'

Ernst Kaltenbrunner

VERDICT: Guilty on counts 3 and 4. Sentenced to death by hanging.

The Judgment against Kaltenbrunner concluded:

'...When he became Chief of the Security Police and SD and head of the RSHA on January 30, 1943, Kaltenbrunner took charge of an organization which included the main offices of the Gestapo, the SD and the Criminal Police... During the period in which Kaltenbrunner was head of the RSHA, it was engaged in a widespread programme of War Crimes and Crimes Against Humanity. These crimes included the mistreatment and murder of prisoners of war. Jews, commissars, and others who were thought to be ideologically hostile to the Nazi regime were reported to the RSHA, which had them transferred to a concentration camp and murdered... The order for the execution of commando troops was extended by the Gestapo to include parachutists while

Kaltenbrunner was Chief of the RSHA. An order signed by Kaltenbrunner instructed the police not to interfere with attacks on bailed out Allied fliers... The RSHA played a leading part in the "Final Solution" of the Jewish question by the extermination of the Jews. A special section under the Amt IV of the RSHA was established to supervise this programme. Under its direction approximately 6 million Jews were murdered, of which 2 million were killed by the *Einsatzgruppen* and other units of the Security Police. Kaltenbrunner had been informed of the activities of these *Einsatzgruppen* when he was a Higher SS and Police leader, and they continued to function after he had become Chief of the RSHA. The murder of approximately 4 million Jews in concentration camps... was also under the supervision of the RSHA when Kaltenbrunner was head of that organization...'

Before his execution, Ernst Kaltenbrunner said he had 'no knowledge' of any crimes; his actions, he claimed, were on behalf of the German people.

Alfred Rosenberg

VERDICT: **Guilty on all four counts. Sentenced to death by hanging.**

The Judgment against Rosenberg concluded:

'... Recognized as the Party's ideologist, he developed and spread Nazi doctrines in the newspapers *Völkischer Beobachter* and *NS Monatshefte*, which he edited, and in the numerous books he wrote... As head of the APA (Aussenpolitisches Amt – the Nazi foreign policy office), Rosenberg was in charge of an organization whose agents were active in Nazi intrigue in all parts of the world. His own reports, for example, claim that the APA was largely responsible for Romania's joining the Axis. As head of the APA, he played an important part in the preparation and planning of the attack on Norway. Rosenberg bears a major responsibility for the formulation and execution of occupation policies in the Occupied Eastern Territories. He was informed by

Hitler on April 2, 1941, of the coming attack against the Soviet Union, and he agreed to help in the capacity of "Political Adviser"... On July 17, 1941, Hitler appointed Rosenberg Reich Minister for the Eastern Occupied Territories, and publicly charged him with responsibility for civil administration... He helped to formulate the policies of Germanization, exploitation, forced labour, extermination of Jews and opponents of Nazi rule, and he set up an administration which carried them out... Rosenberg had knowledge of the brutal treatment and terror to which the Eastern people were subjected. He directed that the Hague Rules of Land Warfare were not applicable in the Occupied Eastern Territories. He had knowledge of and took an active part in stripping the Eastern Territories of raw materials and foodstuffs, which were all sent to Germany. He stated that feeding the German people was first on the list of claims on the East, and the Soviet people would suffer thereby. His directives provided for the segregation of Jews, ultimately in Ghettos. His subordinates engaged in mass killings of Jews, and his civil administrators considered that cleansing the Eastern Occupied Territories of Jews was necessary... He gave his civil administrators quotas of labourers to be sent to the Reich, which had to be met by whatever means necessary. His signature of approval appears on the order of June 14, 1941, for the *Heu Aktion*, the apprehension of 40,000 to 50,000 youths, aged 10–14, for shipment to the Reich...'

Hans Frank

VERDICT: **Guilty on counts 3 and 4. Sentenced to death by hanging.**

The Judgment against Frank concluded:

'... Frank was appointed Chief Civil Administration Officer for occupied Polish territory... on October 3, 1939, he described the policy which he intended to put into effect by stating: "Poland shall be treated like a colony; the Poles will become the slaves of the Greater German World Empire." The evidence establishes that this occupation policy was based on the complete destruction of Poland as a national entity, and a ruthless exploitation of its human and economic resources for the German war effort... Frank was a willing and knowing participant in the use of terrorism in Poland; in the economic exploitation of Poland in a way which led to the death by starvation of a large number of people; in the deportation to Germany as slave labourers of over a million Poles; and in a programme involving the murder of at least 3 million Jews.'

Wilhelm Frick

VERDICT: **Guilty on counts 2, 3 and 4. Sentenced to death by hanging.**

The Judgment against Frick concluded:

'... An avid Nazi, Frick was largely responsible for bringing the German nation under the complete control of the NSDAP... The numerous laws he drafted, signed, and administered abolished all opposition parties and prepared the way for the Gestapo and their concentration camps to extinguish all individual opposition. He was largely responsible for the legislation which suppressed the Trade Unions, the Church, the Jews. He performed this task with ruthless efficiency... Always rabidly anti-Semitic, Frick drafted, signed, and administered many laws destined to eliminate Jews from German life and economy.
His work formed the basis of the Nuremberg Decrees, and he was active in enforcing them... He had knowledge that insane, sick and aged people, "useless eaters," were being systematically put to death. Complaints of these murders reached him, but he did nothing to stop them...'

Wilhelm Frick (standing), giving his final address to the court. He was the only defendant apart from Rudolph Hess to refuse to testify on his own behalf. His last words were 'Long live eternal Germany'.

Julius Streicher

VERDICT: Guilty on count 4. Sentenced to death by hanging.

The Judgment against Streicher concluded:

'... For his 25 years of speaking, writing, and preaching hatred of the Jews, Streicher was widely known as "Jew-Baiter Number One." In his speeches and articles, week after week, month after month, he infected the German mind with the virus of anti-Semitism, and incited the German people to active persecution... Streicher had charge of the Jewish boycott of April 1, 1933. He advocated the Nuremberg Decrees of 1935. IIe was responsible for the demolition on August 10, 1938, of the synagogue in Nuremberg. And on November 10, 1938, he spoke publicly in support of the Jewish pogroms which were taking place at that time. But it was not only in Germany that this defendant advocated his doctrines. As early as 1938 he began to call for the annihilation of the Jewish race... With knowledge of the extermination of the Jews in the Occupied Eastern Territories, this defendant continued to write and publish his propaganda of death... Streicher's incitement to murder and extermination at the time when Jews in the East were being killed under the most horrible conditions clearly constitutes persecution on political and racial grounds in connection with war crimes, as defined by the Charter, and constitutes a crime against humanity.'

Walther Funk

VERDICT: Guilty on counts 2, 3 and 4. Sentenced to life imprisonment.

The Judgment against Funk concluded:

'...Funk became active in the economic field after the Nazi plans to wage aggressive war had been clearly defined... On October 14, 1939, after the war had begun, Funk made a speech in which he stated that the economic and financial departments of Germany working under the Four Year Plan had been engaged in the secret economic preparation for war for over a year... In 1942 Funk entered into an agreement with Himmler under which the Reichsbank was to receive certain gold and jewels and currency from the SS and instructed his subordinates, who were to work out the details, not to ask too many questions. As a result of this agreement the SS sent to the Reichsbank the personal belongings taken from the victims who had been exterminated in the concentration camps. The Reichsbank kept the coins and banknotes and sent the jewels, watches, and personal belongings to Berlin Municipal Pawn Shops. The gold from the eye-glasses and gold teeth and fillings was stored in the Reichsbank vaults. Funk has protested that he did not know that the Reichsbank was receiving articles of this kind. The Tribunal is of the opinion that Funk either knew what was being received or was deliberately closing his eyes to what was being done...'

Hjalmar Schacht

VERDICT: **Not guilty. Schacht was released after which he enjoyed a successful career in international banking. He died in 1970.**

The Judgment for Schacht concluded:

'Schacht was an active supporter of the Nazi Party before its accession to power on January 30, 1933, and supported the appointment of Hitler to the post of Chancellor. After that he played an important role in the vigorous rearmament programme which was adopted, using the facilities of the Reichsbank to the fullest extent in the German rearmament effort... As Minister of Economics and as Plenipotentiary General for War Economy he was active in organizing the German economy for war... But rearmament of itself is not criminal under the Charter. To be a crime against peace under Article 6 of the Charter it must be shown that Schacht carried out this rearmament as part of the Nazi plan to wage aggressive wars... The Tribunal has considered the whole of this evidence with great care, and comes to the conclusion that this necessary inference has not been established beyond a reasonable doubt.'

Hjalmar Schacht (centre) with Adolf Hitler (right) and colleagues. Significant in establishing Schacht's innocence were the facts that he had lost all his important posts before the war began and that he spent the last year of the war as an inmate of Dachau concentration camp.

Karl Doenitz

VERDICT: Guilty on counts 2 and 3. Sentenced to 10 years' imprisonment.

The Judgment against Doenitz concluded:

Karl Doenitz (centre) spent ten years in Spandau Prison. He published his memoirs in 1958.

'Although Doenitz built and trained the German U-boat arm, the evidence does not show he was privy to the conspiracy to wage aggressive wars or that he prepared and initiated such wars... The Tribunal is of the opinion that the evidence does not establish with the certainty required that Doenitz deliberately ordered the killing of shipwrecked survivors... The evidence further shows that the rescue provisions were not carried out and that the defendant ordered that they should not be carried out... Doenitz was also charged with responsibility for Hitler's Commando order of October 18, 1942... [by which] the members of an Allied motor torpedo boat were... turned over to the SD and shot...'

Erich Raeder

**VERDICT: Guilty on counts 1, 2 and 3. Sentenced to life imprisonment.
He was released in 1955.**

The Judgment against Raeder concluded:

'In the 15 years he commanded it, Raeder built and directed the German Navy; he accepts full responsibility until retirement in 1943. He admits the navy violated the Versailles Treaty, insisting it was "a matter of honour for every man" to do so... The conception of the invasion of Norway first arose in the mind of Raeder and not that of Hitler... Raeder endeavoured to dissuade Hitler from embarking upon the invasion of the USSR... But once the decision had been made, he gave permission six days before the invasion of the Soviet Union to attack Russian submarines in the Baltic Sea... It is clear from this evidence that Raeder participated in the planning and waging of aggressive war...'

Baldur von Schirach

VERDICT: **Guilty on count 4. Sentenced to 20 years' imprisonment.**

The Judgment against von Schirach concluded:

'...Von Schirach used the Hitler Youth to educate German Youth "in the spirit of National Socialism" and subjected them to an extensive programme of Nazi propaganda...When von Schirach became *Gauleiter* of Vienna the deportation of the Jews had already begun... On September 15, 1942, von Schirach made a speech in which he defended his action in having driven "tens of thousands upon tens of thousands of Jews into the Ghetto of the East" as "contributing to European culture"...The Tribunal finds that von Schirach, while he did not originate the policy of deporting Jews from Vienna, participated in this deportation after he had become *Gauleiter* of Vienna. He knew that the best the Jews could hope for was a miserable existence in the Ghettos of the East. Bulletins describing the Jewish extermination were in his office...'

Von Schirach served his 20-year sentence in Spandau Prison. His wife divorced him in 1949.

Fritz Sauckel

VERDICT: **Guilty on counts 3 and 4. Sentenced to death by hanging.**

The Judgment against Sauckel concluded:

'... Shortly after Sauckel had taken office, he had the governing authorities in the various occupied territories issue decrees, establishing compulsory labour service in Germany...That real voluntary recruiting was the exception rather than the rule is shown by Sauckel's statement on March 1, 1944 that "out of 5 million workers who arrived in Germany, not even 200,000 came voluntarily."... His attitude was thus expressed in a regulation: "All the men must be fed, sheltered, and treated in such a way as to exploit them to the highest possible extent at the lowest conceivable degree of expenditure." The evidence shows that Sauckel was in charge of a programme which involved deportation for slave labour of more than 5 million human beings, many of them under terrible conditions of cruelty and suffering.'

Alfred Jodl

VERDICT: **Guilty on all 4 counts. Sentenced to death by hanging.**

The Judgment against Jodl concluded:

'... Jodl discussed the Norway invasion with Hitler, Keitel, and Raeder on December 12, 1939; his diary is replete with late entries on his activities in preparing this attack... He was active in the planning against Greece and Yugoslavia... Jodl testified that Hitler feared an attack by Russia and so attacked first. This preparation began almost a year before the invasion. Jodl told Warlimont as early as July 29, 1940 to prepare the plans since Hitler had decided to attack... A plan to eliminate Soviet commissars was in the directive for "Case Barbarossa". The decision whether they should be killed without trial was to be made by an officer... His defence, in brief, is the doctrine of "superior orders," prohibited by Article 8 of the Charter as a defence... Participation in such crimes as these has never been required of any soldier and he cannot now shield himself behind a mythical requirement of soldierly obedience at all costs as his excuse for commission of these crimes.'

Franz von Papen
VERDICT: **Not guilty. Acquitted.**

The Judgment for von Papen concluded:

'Von Papen was active in 1932 and 1933 in helping Hitler to form the Coalition Cabinet and aided in his appointment as Chancellor on January 30, 1933. As Vice-Chancellor in that Cabinet he participated in the Nazi consolidation of control in 1933... Notwithstanding the murder of his associates, von Papen accepted the position of Minister to Austria on July 26, 1934, the day after Dollfuss had been assassinated... The evidence leaves no doubt that von Papen's primary purpose as Minister to Austria was to undermine the Schuschnigg regime and strengthen the Austrian Nazis for the purpose of bringing about the Anschluss. To carry through this plan he engaged in both intrigue and bullying. But the Charter does not make criminal such offences against political morality, however bad these may be... Under the Charter, von Papen can be held guilty only if he was party to the planning of aggressive war... but it is not established beyond a reasonable doubt that this was the purpose of his activity...'

Franz von Papen (right) discussing details of his case with his son, Franz von Papen Jnr. His son acted as his second defence counsel at the trial.

Arthur Seyss-Inquart

VERDICT: **Guilty on counts 2, 3 and 4. Sentenced to death by hanging.**

The Judgment against Seyss-Inquart concluded:

'... Seyss-Inquart participated in the last stages of the Nazi intrigue which preceded the German occupation of Austria... As Reich Commissioner for the Occupied Netherlands, Seyss-Inquart was ruthless in applying terrorism to suppress all opposition to the German occupation, a programme which he described as "annihilating" his opponents. In collaboration with the Higher SS and Police leaders he was involved in the shooting of hostages for offences against the occupation authorities and sending to concentration camps all suspected opponents of occupation policies including priests and educators... Seyss-Inquart contends that he was not responsible for many of the crimes committed in the occupation of the Netherlands... But the fact remains that Seyss-Inquart was a knowing and voluntary participant in War Crimes and Crimes against Humanity which were committed in the occupation of the Netherlands.'

Albert Speer

VERDICT: Guilty on counts 3 and 4. Sentenced to 20 years' imprisonment. On his release in 1966, he published his memoirs, *Inside the Third Reich*, which became a bestseller. He died in 1981.

The Judgment against Speer concluded:

Albert Speer planning the construction of a new Germany with his mentor, Adolf Hitler.

'The evidence introduced against Speer under counts 3 and 4 relates entirely to his participation in the slave labour programme... As Reich Minister for Armaments and Munitions and General Plenipotentiary for Armaments under the Four Year Plan, Speer had extensive authority over production... The practice was developed under which Speer transmitted to Sauckel an estimate of the total number of workers needed, Sauckel obtained the labour and allocated it to the various industries in accordance with instructions supplied by Speer. Speer knew when he made his demands on Sauckel that they would be supplied by foreign labourers serving under compulsion... Sauckel continually informed Speer and his representative that foreign labourers were being obtained by force...'

Konstantin von Neurath

VERDICT: Guilty on all 4 counts. Sentenced to 15 years' imprisonment. Released after 8 years on grounds of ill health.

The Judgment against von Neurath concluded:

'...Von Neurath was appointed Reich Protector for Bohemia and Moravia on March 18, 1939... The free press, political parties, and trade unions were abolished. All groups which might serve as opposition were outlawed... He served as the chief German official in the Protectorate when the administration of this territory played an important role in the wars of aggression which Germany was waging in the East, knowing that War Crimes and Crimes Against Humanity were being committed under his authority...'

Konstantin von Neurath was sentenced to 15 years' imprisonment, but was released from Spandau Prison in 1954 having suffered a heart attack. He died in Enzweihingen in 1956.

Hans Fritzsche

VERDICT: **Not guilty. Acquitted.**

The Judgment for Fritzsche concluded:

'...The Radio Division, of which Fritzsche became the head in November 1942, was one of the twelve divisions of the Propaganda Ministry... It appears that Fritzsche sometimes made strong statements of a propagandistic nature in his broadcasts. But the Tribunal is not prepared to hold that they were intended to incite the German people to commit atrocities on conquered peoples, and he cannot be said to have been a participant in the crimes charged...'

Although acquitted at Nuremberg, Hans Fritzsche was subsequently sentenced to nine years by a West German denazification court.

181

The three acquitted defendants, Franz von Pappen, Hjalmar Schacht and Hans Fritzsche, can't believe their luck at a press conference attended by journalists from all over the world. But their ordeal was far from over.

Acquitted but Unwanted

Having been acquitted, Fritzsche, Schacht and von Papen were free to go. While their fellow defendants awaited sentencing back in their cells the three attended a hastily convened press conference at which they breathlessly expressed their joy and surprise at the leniency that had been shown to them.

Their delight was shortlived. Within hours of the verdict being announced a hostile crowd gathered at the gates of the courthouse calling for the three Nazis to be lynched. The tide had turned against the former masters, who were forced to spend another night in the cells for their own safety while the authorities discussed ways of smuggling them out. Two days later Fritzsche and Schacht were taken to a secret location elsewhere in the city, while von Papen waited in his cell for another three weeks until his son came to take him home. They did not know that they would later be brought before a German court, where they would be found guilty on lesser charges and be given nominal prison sentences.

Sentencing

Shortly before 3 pm on 1 October the remaining defendants returned to the court from the cell block to hear the sentences. A doctor and a nurse were in attendance and a stretcher was placed in the lift that would take each man into the dock for the last time. Colonel Andrus told the guilty men that it was their duty to themselves, to posterity and to the German people to conduct themselves with dignity and to stand to attention while the sentence was being read. They should then retire quietly and without comment. The bright lights were dimmed because no cameras were present – the press and the public were also excluded.

Prison psychologist Dr G.M. Gilbert was privy to the defendants' immediate reactions on being sentenced. He recorded his observations in his diary.

'Goering came down first and strode into his cell, his face pale and frozen, his eyes popping. "Death!" he said as he dropped on the cot and reached for a book. His hands were trembling in spite of his attempt to be nonchalant. His eyes were moist and he was panting, fighting back an emotional breakdown. He asked me in an unsteady voice to leave him alone for a while.'

Later Goering confessed that he had expected the death penalty. In fact, he truthfully preferred it to a life sentence, because only the dead become martyrs. But there was nothing of his former arrogance in his voice when he said those words.

Hess laughed nervously and declared that he had not even been listening, so he did not know what the sentence was. What was more, he did not care. His only question was why he had been handcuffed, unlike Goering, but he guessed it was because he had been given a life sentence while Goering had been sentenced to death.

Gilbert found Ribbentrop pacing his cell in a daze. He was whispering to himself.

'Death! – Death! Now I won't be able to write my beautiful memoirs. Tsk! Tsk! So much hatred! Tsk! tsk!'

Ribbentrop then slumped down on his bed and stared blankly into space.

When Gilbert entered Keitel's cell the former field marshal wheeled around and snapped to attention. His fists were clenched and his arms were rigid. There was a startled look of utter disbelief in his eyes.

'Death – by hanging!' he repeated. 'That, at least, I thought I would be spared. I don't blame you for standing at a distance from a man sentenced to death by hanging. I understand that perfectly. But I am still the same as before. If you will please only – visit me sometimes in these last days.'

Dr Gilbert promised that he would.

Frank smiled politely, but could not meet Dr Gilbert's gaze.

'Death by hanging,' he said softly, nodding his head in acquiescence. 'I deserved it and I expected it, as I've always told you. I am glad that I have had the chance to defend myself and to think things over in the last few months.'

Doenitz was dumbfounded, but said he was sure his American counterpart Admiral Nimitz 'understood him perfectly'.

Jodl marched defiantly to his cell as if to face a firing squad. He too avoided Gilbert's eyes. His face was flushed and he spoke in broken sentences as if struggling to find the right words.

'Death by hanging! That, at least, I did not deserve. The death part – all right, somebody has to stand for the responsibility. But that – that I did not deserve.'

His mouth quivered and his voice broke with the shame of it.

Gilbert found Speer in characteristically good spirits. He laughed nervously.

'Twenty years. Well; that's fair enough. They couldn't have given me a lighter sentence, considering the facts, and I can't complain. I said the sentences must be severe, and I admitted my share of the guilt, so it would be ridiculous if I complained about the punishment.'

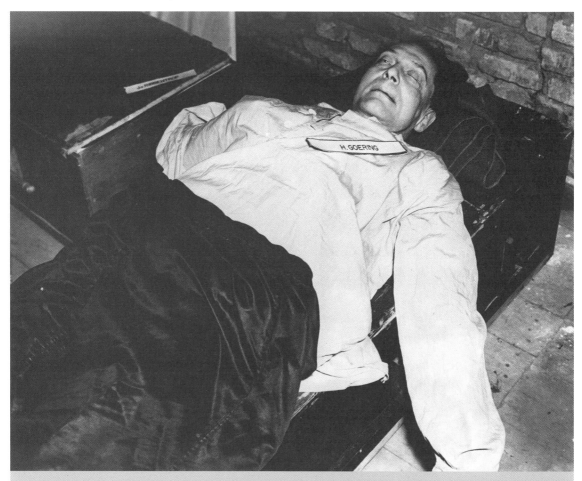

Dressed in black silk pyjamas under his blue shirt, Goering swallowed a cyanide capsule, then died in agony. His body was exhibited to correspondents so no myth could grow up that he had escaped alive.

Goering Cheats the Hangman

The condemned men had to endure an agonizing two-week wait before their execution, the date of which was kept from them until the last moment.

Goering, however, had no intention of submitting to Allied justice. He had participated in the trial to ensure his place in history and he could even have entertained the unrealistic hope that he might have been sentenced to life imprisonment. But once the death sentence had been passed and all appeals for clemency had been refused by the Allied Control Commission, there were only two decisions remaining – how and when he would take his own life.

On the evening of 16 October, Goering's impressionable young GI guard responded to his avuncular charm by returning his personal belongings without properly checking them. There was no reason to think that one of the items, a small bag of toiletries, contained the means by which the condemned man would cheat the hangman. But concealed among Goering's personal belongings was a capsule containing potassium cyanide. Two hours before his execution he slipped it into his mouth and bit into it. Within minutes he had died an agonizing death that left his face contorted with pain. He left a suicide note addressed to his wife, in which he confessed that he would not have objected to a firing squad, but death by hanging was an undignified exit for a soldier.

The Final Act

Just after 1 am on that same night, von Ribbentrop was taken from his cell in manacles and marched to the gymnasium that had been built in the courtyard. As he entered he was seized firmly by two Army sergeants, while another guard replaced the manacles with a leather strap, which pinned his arms to his sides.

Ribbentrop did not protest as his guards propelled him to the foot of the scaffold on which he would end his days. It was one of three that had been erected in the room – two were to be used alternately and the third was a spare, in the unlikely event of any technical problems. After mounting the steps to the platform, he was asked to confirm his name. He did not answer at first, but when the question was repeated he shouted, 'Joachim von Ribbentrop!' as if he were reporting to the gatekeeper at the entrance to Valhalla. Then he turned to face the witnesses. When he was asked if he had a final message he said:

'God protect Germany. My last wish is that Germany realize its unity and that an understanding be reached between the East and the West. I wish peace to the world.'

The black hood was placed in position on his head, the hangman pulled the lever and von Ribbentrop plunged beneath the trapdoor.

Two minutes later, while the rope was still quivering, Keitel entered the room and was dispatched with the same silent efficiency on the adjacent gallows. He, too, held his head proudly and met his fate with composure. His last words were:

'I call on God Almighty to have mercy on the German people. More than 2 million German soldiers went to their death for the fatherland before me. I follow now my sons. Germany over all!'

Kaltenbrunner could not bring himself to admit his guilt so he did not ask forgiveness, even in the hour of his death. He made a defiant speech from the scaffold in a firm voice.

'I have loved my German people with a warm heart. And my Fatherland. I have done my duty by the laws of my people and I regret that my people were led this time by men who were not soldiers and that crimes were committed of which I have no knowledge.'

Rosenberg said nothing, for nothing could excuse the man who had been the author of the message of hate, murder and racism that had underpinned the Nazi ideology.

Hans Frank was next. In spite of the forced smile on his face he was clearly battling his nerves. He swallowed frequently as he confirmed his name in an undertone and his last statement was difficult to catch.

'I am thankful for the kind treatment during my captivity and I ask God to accept me with mercy.'

Streicher had refused to put on his civilian clothes so he had been forcibly dressed by the guards. He was manhandled to the gallows screaming, 'Heil Hitler!' and he cursed the hangman, warning him that he would one day be hanged by the Communists. His last words were a reference to the hanging of a Jew-baiter in the 5th century.

'Purim Fest 1946!'

Sauckel, in contrast, went meekly to his death, muttering incoherently about the injustice of the sentence that had condemned him to death, while his master, Speer, had escaped with a 20-year prison sentence.

Jodl entered the death chamber an hour and a half after the executions had begun, wetting his lips to ensure his voice would not crack when he came to say his last words. His face was as drawn and dry as parchment as he walked unsteadily to the steps of the scaffold. His last words were

'My greetings to you, my Germany.'

Seyss-Inquart addressed the witnesses in a weak voice.

'I hope that this execution is the last act of the tragedy of the Second World War, and I hope that out of this disaster wisdom will inspire the people which will result in understanding between the nations and that peace on earth will finally be established.'

Then he, too, dropped into oblivion.

The last of the condemned men to be brought in was Hermann Goering, whose body was carried on a stretcher covered by a khaki-coloured army blanket. He might have cheated the hangman, but it was necessary for his death to be recorded and photographed for posterity. The blanket was drawn back for the benefit of the witnesses who saw that Goering's black silk pyjama jacket was soaking from the prison doctor's frantic efforts to revive him. His face was contorted in pain. The body was covered and the witnesses filed out.

Just before dawn the bodies were taken away in two trucks under heavy guard and driven to Dachau concentration camp, a short distance northwest of Munich, where the ovens had been relit for their cremation. The ashes were scattered in a nearby river.

There was no sense of triumph among the victors, only relief that this tragic and violent era had finally come to an end.

CHAPTER SIX

THE FORGOTTEN TRIALS

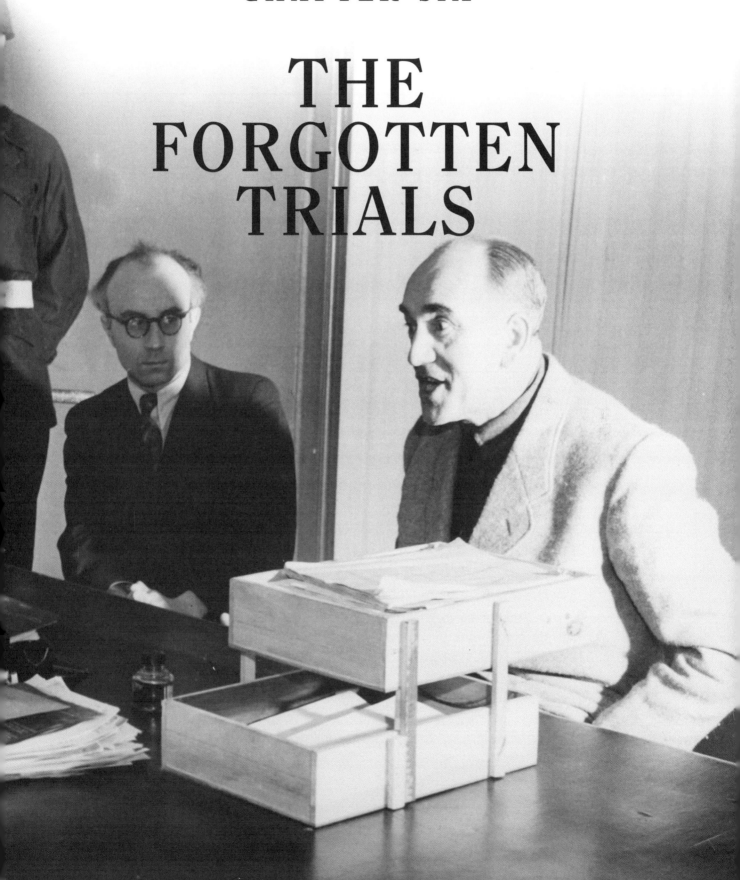

Professor Dr Wilhelm Beiglebōck (second left, from top) was Consulting Physician to the Luftwaffe and performed medical 'tests' involving seawater on inmates of Dachau concentration camp. He pleaded not guilty but was sentenced to 10 years. He is seen seated here with members of both the prosecuting and defending judicial teams.

The trial of the major Nazi war criminals was not the only tribunal to be held in Nuremberg in the immediate postwar period, but it was the only hearing at which all four of the Allied powers were represented. Shortly after the main trial ended, 12 further trials were held by the Americans. They took place at the Palace of Justice because Nuremberg was in the American zone of occupation. As a result, they became known as the 'Subsequent Nuremberg Trials'.

Although these trials did not capture the headlines, they were no less significant for what they revealed of the murderous mentality of the Nazi minions. The fact that they were held at all demonstrated that the Allies were determined to pursue justice for the victims, even if the press and the public had tired of atrocity stories. But these were all-American affairs. The Russians held their own trials of captured Nazis and their associates in Moscow while other nations, including West Germany, conducted their prosecutions periodically during the Cold War period and beyond.

⚖

The Doctors' Trial

9 December 1946 – 20 August 1947

The doctors' trial opened in Nuremberg on 9 December 1946 and ended on 20 August 1947. Chief Judge Walter Beals of the Supreme Court of the State of Washington presided.

Twenty-three defendants were arraigned including Karl Brandt, who had been one of Hitler's personal physicians. Brandt, a major-general in the SS, held the most senior medical post in the Reich, with authority over all military and civilian medical services. His fellow defendants included Lieutenant-General Siegfried Handloser (the Army's chief medical officer), Lieutenant-General Oscar Schroeder (chief of the medical service of the Luftwaffe), and Major-General Karl Gebhardt (chief surgeon of the SS and president of the German Red Cross).

According to the indictment, these men and their subordinates had performed sadistic 'medical experiments' on concentration camp inmates and prisoners of war. The victims of the defendants had been subjected to the effects of high altitude; immersed in freezing water; exposed to mustard gas; forced to drink seawater; sterilized involuntarily; and purposely wounded by incendiary bombs. Prisoners were also injected with potentially fatal viruses such as malaria and typhus, under the pretext that the doctors were testing the effectiveness of the vaccines. Finally, bullets laced with poison were fired into inmates to see how swiftly the poison would act on a wounded victim. In all of these cases there was not even the pretence of finding an antidote. But perhaps the most macabre incident of all was that of the 112 Jewish concentration camp inmates who were murdered for their skeletons, in order to complete the anatomy collection at the University of Strasbourg.

Karl Brandt was sentenced to death by hanging, which was carried out on 2 June 1948.

At the trial it was alleged that the German medical profession participated in the genocide of Jews and other 'undesirables' – specifically at the selection process in the camps, when new inmates were chosen for forced labour or the gas chambers. During the proceedings it was also stated that as early as 1929 the Nazi Physicians' League had been established. One of its aims had been to bring about the expulsion of Jewish doctors from the medical community. By 1942, more than 38,000 doctors were said to be members of the Nazi Party.

When the court asked Auschwitz doctor Fritz Klein how he could reconcile his oath to preserve life with his actions at the camp, he answered:

'Of course I am a doctor and I want to preserve life. And out of *respect* for human life, I would remove a gangrenous appendix from a diseased body. The *Jew* is the gangrenous appendix in the body of mankind.'

After more than seven months, during which 85 witnesses had testified and 1,471 documents had been entered in evidence, the Tribunal concluded:

'Judged by any standard of proof the record clearly shows the commission of war crimes and crimes against humanity substantially as alleged in counts two and three of the indictment. Beginning with the outbreak of World War II criminal medical experiments on non-German nationals, both prisoners of war and civilians, including Jews and "asocial" persons, were carried out on a large scale in Germany and the occupied countries.'

Sixteen of the 23 defendants were subsequently found guilty. Seven were sentenced to death by hanging, nine received prison terms ranging from 10 years to life and a further seven were acquitted. The executions were carried out in Landsberg Prison, where Hitler had dictated the first volume of *Mein Kampf* to secretary Rudolf Hess in 1924.

The Milch Trial

2 January – 16 April 1947

Former German field marshal Erhard Milch was charged with murder, the inhumane treatment of prisoners of war and participating in medical experiments. Milch was found guilty and sentenced to imprisonment for life.

Erhard Milch stands to receive his life sentence. Seated to his left is his attorney, Dr Friedrich Bergold.

The Judges' Trial

5 March – 4 December 1947

Nine members of the Reich Ministry of Justice and seven members of the People's and Special Courts were charged with abusing their power as prosecutors and judges to commit war crimes and crimes against humanity, which had led to the false imprisonment and death of unnamed innocents.

> 'The defendants are charged with crimes of such immensity that mere specific instances of criminality appear insignificant by comparison. The charge, in brief, is that of conscious participation in a nationwide government-organized system of cruelty and injustice, in violation of the laws of war and humanity, and perpetrated in the name of law by the authority of the Ministry of Justice, and through the instrumentality of the courts. The dagger of the assassin was concealed beneath the robe of the jurist. The record is replete with evidence of specific criminal acts, but they are not the crimes charged in the indictment… No indictment couched in specific terms and in the manner of common law could have encompassed within practicable limits the generality of the offence with which these defendants stand charged.'

In his opening statement, Brigadier-General Telford Taylor accused the defendants of subverting the law to serve an evil administration.

> 'In summary, the defendants are charged with the judicial murder and other atrocities which they committed by destroying law and justice in Germany, and by then utilizing the emptied forms of legal process for persecution, enslavement, and extermination under law. The true purposes of this proceeding, therefore, are broader than the mere visiting of retribution on a few men for the death and suffering of many thousands… Great as was their crime against those who died or suffered at their hands, their crime against Germany was even more shameful. They defiled the German temple of justice, and delivered Germany into the dictatorship of the Third Reich, "with all its methods of terror, and its cynical and open denial of the rule of law".'

The cases of Nazi injustice heard by the court were numerous, but one case in particular helped seal the fate of the accused.

Leo Katzenberger was a Jewish businessman who had seen his chain of shoe stores stolen from him by the Nazis under the Aryanization decrees of 1938, which legalized theft from German Jews. The elderly man had no hope of emigrating so he continued to live in an apartment in one of his properties. During 1941 his friendship with a teenage girl, Irene Seiler, was reported to the authorities, who accused Katzenberger of violating the race laws, which forbade relationships between Aryans and Jews. At his trial, 67-year-old Katzenberger repeatedly denied that there was anything of a sexual nature in the relationship, but his protests were shouted down by the presiding judge, Dr Oswald Rothaug, who called Katzenberger a 'syphilitic Jew' and 'an agent of world Jewry'. Katzenberger was sentenced to death.

During the Judges' Trial it was stated that jurists and prosecutors could not refuse to implement Nazi laws without jeopardizing their lives, but that defence was dismissed when the prosecution raised the case of a Brandenburg judge, Dr Lothar Kreyssig, who had refused to dispense Nazi justice. When Kreyssig learned that patients at his local hospital were being murdered with the tacit approval of their doctors he wrote to the Prussian Supreme Court. His complaint was ignored, so he issued injunctions against the hospital and brought charges against one of the administrators of the programme. He refused to back down when asked, but after being threatened with incarceration in a concentration camp he was forced to take early retirement. The Kreyssig and the Katzenberger cases were both dramatized for the film *Judgment At Nuremberg* (1961), which was based on the Judges' Trial.

The trial ended with ten defendants being convicted and four being acquitted. Another respondent was freed on a technicality and one of the accused died before the verdict could be reached.

The American and the West German authorities expressed unease about the stiff sentences, especially those handed down to the former judges Tothaug and Oeschey, who had been imprisoned for life. Their sentences were subsequently reduced to 20 years. By 1951, however, only one former defendant remained in prison. Rothaug was finally released in 1956 and died a free man in 1967.

Oswald Rothaug, who had been known as the 'hanging judge', was sentenced to life, but was released in 1956 and died in 1967.

The WVHA Trial

8 April – 3 November 1947

'In no way am I responsible or guilty for the murder of the 5 million Jews or the deaths of others in the concentration camps... The fact that I was in charge of all the concentration camps in Germany from 1942 until the end is beside the point.'

OSWALD POHL

SS Lieutenant-General Oswald Pohl and 17 other officials of the WVHA (the Economic and Administrative Office of the SS) were charged with crimes relating to the construction and administration of the thousands of concentration camps in Germany and the occupied countries. The WVHA also profited from the mines, quarries and brick factories in which the prisoners were forced to work.

Other charges grew out of the organized looting of personal property owned by the Jews who had been sent to the camps. The stolen goods were not limited to valuables but included beds, blankets and even perambulators. It was estimated that the total theft was in the region of 100 million Reichmarks.

Oswald Pohl (far right) had direct control over the organization of concentration camps and the distribution of slave labour during the war. After several failed appeals, he was hanged in June 1951.

Judge Robert Toms of the Circuit Court of Michigan presided. Pohl and three other defendants were sentenced to death by hanging, a further 11 respondents received prison terms ranging from 10 years to life and three were acquitted.

Judge Robert M. Toms (centre), presiding judge of the secondary military tribunals at Nuremberg, alights from his car outside the Palace of Justice to be greeted by Colonel Charles W. May (left), marshall of all the courts.

In summing up the case the tribunal concluded:

'Under the spell of National Socialism, these defendants today are only mildly conscious of any guilt in the kidnapping and enslavement of millions of civilians. The concept that slavery is criminal per se does not enter into their thinking. Their attitude may be summarized thus:

'We fed and clothed and housed those prisoners as best we could. If they were hungry and cold, so were the Germans. If they had to work long hours under trying conditions, so did the Germans. What is wrong with that?

'The electrically charged wire, the armed guards, the vicious dogs, the sentinel towers – all those are blandly explained by saying, "Why, of course. Otherwise the inmates would have run away." They simply cannot realize that the most precious word in any language is "liberty".

'Slavery may exist even without torture. Slaves may be well fed and well clothed and comfortably housed, but they are still slaves if without lawful process they are deprived of their freedom by forceful restraint. We might eliminate all proof of ill treatment, overlook the starvation and beatings and other barbarous acts, but the admitted fact of slavery – compulsory uncompensated labour – would still remain. There is no such thing as benevolent slavery. Involuntary servitude, even if tempered by humane treatment, is still slavery.'

The Flick Trial

19 April – 22 December 1947

Six members of the Flick Cartel, an association of industrial concerns, were charged with using slave labour and prisoners of war, deporting persons for labour in Geman-occupied territories and stealing private property – the so called 'Aryanization' of Jewish businesses. Friedrich Flick and two fellow defendants were convicted and sent to prison. Three others were acquitted.

The Hostage Case

15 July 1947 – 19 February 1948

Twelve German officers were indicted on charges of murdering civilians in Albania, Greece and Yugoslavia; committing 'acts of devastation' in Norway and other countries; denying prisoners of war their rights under the Geneva Convention; and ordering the murder of surrendered troops. Two defendants committed suicide before the verdict was reached. Eight others were sentenced to long terms of imprisonment and two were acquitted.

The IG Farben Trial

27 August 1947 – 30 July 1948

Heinrich Buetefisch, former secretary of Farben's governing body and head of production at Auschwitz, testifies below charts of IG Farben's Morschburg plant. He was sentenced to six years and died in 1969.

Twenty-four employees of IG Farben were charged with the theft of private property in German-occupied territories, together with other war crimes. Judge Hebert argued that the defence of 'necessity' was inapplicable in this case.

'Willing co-operation with the slave labour utilization of the Third Reich was a matter of corporate policy that permeated the whole Farben organization… For this reason, criminal responsibility goes beyond the actual immediate participants at Auschwitz. It includes other Farben Vorstand plant-managers and embraces all who knowingly participated in the shaping of the corporate policy.'

But his was the dissenting voice on the bench. His fellow judges were more lenient and set ten of the defendants free. The remainder were found guilty on one or more charges. They were then imprisoned, but the sentences were comparatively light.

The *Einsatzgruppen* Trial

29 September 1947 – 9 April 1948

The *Einsatzgruppen* were mobile death squads who followed in the wake of the Wehrmacht's advances in Russia. Their task was to eliminate all Communist Party members, gypsies and Jews without mercy.

Although it receded into obscurity, it could be argued that this was the largest single murder trial in legal history, because the victims numbered more than a million.

The 24 defendants were all senior officers, whose defence dragged on for five months. By contrast, the prosecution case had taken a mere two days to present all the pertinent facts.

The tribunal declared that these facts were so incredible that...

'... only the most complete judicial inquiry, and the most exhaustive trial, could verify and confirm them... The charge of purposeful homicide in this case reaches such fantastic proportions and surpasses such credible limits that believability must be bolstered with assurance a hundred times repeated.'

Surprisingly, each defendant was well educated and knew full well what they were being ordered to do. Eight were lawyers, one was a university professor, a third was an opera singer and a fourth had been an art collector; yet they were shown to have been capable of the most brutal crimes of modern times.

As in the earlier trials, the defendants were damned by their own hand. They had made detailed reports regarding their activities which even they could not deny in court.

SS Major-General Otto Ohlendorf had been the commander of *Einsatzgruppen D*, which had been responsible for the murder of 90,000 Jews in the Ukraine and the Crimea, many of them children. On the stand he declared that he was not ashamed of killing them because it was a 'necessity' that could be justified on military grounds.

Otto Ohlendorf told his prosecutor that he was not ashamed of having murdered children.

'I believe that it is very simple to explain if one starts from the fact this order did not only try to achieve security but also a *permanent* security; for that reason the children were people who would grow up and surely, being the children of parents who had been killed, they would constitute a danger no smaller than that of the parents.'

The Tribunal sentenced Ohlendorf and 13 of his fellow defendants to death by hanging. Two others were sentenced to life imprisonment, and five more were sent to prison for periods of between 10 and 20 years. There were no acquittals.

The RuSHA Trial

29 October 1947 – 10 March 1948

Fourteen officials in the Race and Settlement Office and the Office for the Strengthening of Germanism were charged with crimes against humanity in respect of the deportation, torture and murder of foreign nationals. Thirteen defendants were found guilty on one or more charges and sentenced to terms of imprisonment. One was acquitted.

The Krupp Trial

8 December 1947 – 31 July 1948

Twelve directors and senior employees of Krupp Industries – including Alfried Krupp, son of Gustav Krupp – were charged with war crimes and enslavement. Eleven were found guilty on one or more charges. They were sentenced to various terms of imprisonment ranging from 3 to 12 years. One was acquitted.

The 38-year-old Alfried Krupp seated on an American jeep after his capture. Released from prison in 1953, he quickly regained his vast fortune and became a prominent German philanthropist.

Alfried Krupp justified his role in the rearmament of Germany, in defiance of the Treaty of Versailles, by saying:

'**We Krupps never cared much for [political] ideas. We only wanted a system that worked well and allowed us to work unhindered. Politics is not our business.**'

The justices were not convinced and in their Judgment they concluded:

'**This huge octopus, the Krupp Firm, with its body at Essen, swiftly unfolded one of its tentacles behind each new aggressive push of the Wehrmacht... That this growth and expansion on the part of the Krupp Firm was due in large measure to the favoured position it held with Hitler there can be little doubt. The close relationship between Krupp on the one hand and the Reich Government, particularly the Army and Navy Command, on the other hand, amounted to a veritable alliance. The wartime activities of the Krupp concern were based in part upon exploitation of other countries and on exploitation and maltreatment of large masses of forced foreign labour.**'

Alfried was sentenced to 12 years' imprisonment and ordered to forfeit his property. The Krupp factory was dismantled and its machinery was dispersed around the world. However, Alfried was released early, in 1953, and he was soon back in business. By 1960 Krupp Industries had a turnover of 300 million pounds.

The High Command Trial

30 December 1947 – 28 October 1948

The accused were high-ranking Wehrmacht generals, members of the German High Command (OKW) and one former admiral. All were charged with having planned or participated in numerous atrocities. Of the 14 defendants indicted, two were acquitted on all counts.

The Ministries Trial

6 January 1948 – 13 April 1949

Twenty-one members of the Nazi administration, including three ministers, were charged with waging wars of aggression, violating international treaties and crimes against humanity. Nineteen were found guilty on one or more charges. They were sentenced to between 4 and 25 years' imprisonment.

Epilogue

The Nuremberg Legacy

Brigadier-General Telford Taylor, who served as the chief prosecutor at each of the 12 Subsequent Trials, summed up their significance in an interview for the International News Service, shortly after the proceedings were concluded.

> **'The Nuremberg trials, like all judicial trials, must be something more than an episode; they must be part of a process. Nuremberg was part of the process of enforcing law – law that long antedated the trials, and that will endure into the future, law that binds not only Germans or Japanese, but all men. As the Nuremberg Tribunal itself declared in the last judgment:**

> **'We may not, in justice, apply to these defendants because they are German, standards of duty and responsibility which are not equally applicable to the officials of the Allied Powers and to those of all nations. Nor should Germans be convicted for acts or conduct which, if committed by Americans, British, French, or Russians would not subject them to legal trial and conviction.'**

Telford Taylor disagreed with those who were concerned that Nuremberg had established a dangerous precedent.

> **'As a rule, these anxieties spring from the notion that at Nuremberg the Nazi diplomats were punished for drafting notes, the generals for making military plans, and the businessmen for manufacturing war materials – things that were done by our own diplomats and generals and businessmen… No Nuremberg defendant was accused or convicted merely because he held a high position or performed a particular function, but only upon a showing that he used or abused the position, authority, or skill in a criminal manner.'**

The doctors had been indicted because they had performed 'murderous medical experiments' on unwilling prisoners; the industrialists had been placed on trial because they had engaged in the enslavement of millions of foreign civilians and had done nothing to improve the inhumane conditions in which these people were forced to live; and the German generals and diplomats had been arraigned because they willingly participated in the extermination of racial and religious minorities.

'It was these and other such acts that underlie the Nuremberg judgments, and the only precedent that Nuremberg has established is that these crimes may be punished by internationally-constituted courts... It is a precedent which will be welcomed by all who believe that peace and human dignity will find their guarantees in the establishment of world order under the rule of law.'

TELFORD TAYLOR PAPERS, COLUMBIA UNIVERSITY LAW SCHOOL, NEW YORK (9 MAY 1949)

The Importance of the Nuremberg Trials

The Nuremberg Trials did not make the world a safer place, nor did they eradicate injustice, racial and religious persecution, enslavement, torture or genocide. However, the trials did establish a precedent for the prosecution and punishment of those responsible for the sort of crimes that the international community considers intolerable – wherever and by whomever they might be committed. After Nuremberg, no head of state could claim to be above the law and individuals could not evade their responsibilities by hiding behind the anonymity of the administration they had served. Ethnic cleansing, the waging of aggressive war and the evils attendant on those crimes are now punishable under international law. We now have clear codes of conduct where once there was uncertainty and ambiguity. Military personnel can no longer claim that they were forced to commit crimes under duress, nor can they fall back on the defence that they were duty bound to obey superior orders.

Without the Nuremberg Trials there would have been no legal framework on which to base the prosecution of those individuals who were responsible for the atrocities in the former Yugoslavia, in Rwanda and in Sierra Leone. Also, the trials of tyrants such as Slobodan Milosevic and Saddam Hussein would never have taken place.

The Nuremberg Trials laid the foundation for the international human rights laws, which entitle every human being to apply to the courts if they feel that their rights have been violated. But their more immediate effect was to bring to account those responsible for instigating the Second World War in Europe. The trials also gave those who had suffered and survived the opportunity to have their experiences recorded for posterity. Perhaps just as importantly, the events of Nuremberg have served to inform warmongers the world over that they will be punished if they violate international treaties in their treatment of prisoners and civilians. Before the Nuremberg Trials there existed no legislation governing the conduct of war.

The lessons of Nuremberg are not invalidated, as some might argue, by the subsequent atrocities and abuses committed by the United States in Vietnam and Iraq, by the British in Northern Ireland, by the French in Algeria and by the Russians in Afghanistan and in their satellite states. Any abuses that took place in these countries are also covered by the laws that were formulated and clarified in postwar Germany and no right-thinking person would deny a captured enemy the right to humane treatment, be they freedom fighter or terrorist. The fact that these abuses continue is not the fault of those who prosecuted and presided at the Nuremberg tribunals. The torture, imprisonment without trial and ethnic cleansing that we witness on the nightly news does not expose the flaws in international law, only our ability and willingness to enforce it.

Laws exist to discourage the commitment of criminal acts and to punish those responsible when proof has been produced beyond a reasonable doubt. Thanks to those who convened the Nuremberg trials, the deterrent exists. It is the determination to implement the law that is often lacking.

The Nuremberg trials offered some form of closure to the citizens of war-torn Europe – even though numerous Nazis and their collaborators escaped, while others convinced themselves that they were not guilty at all. But justice is subjective and no law is perfect. The very nature of laws is that they are ever-evolving – they are constantly adapting to the world and the societies they serve. The alternative to Nuremberg would have been the summary execution of the Nazi leaders. This might have satisfied the immediate need for vengeance, but the wrong message would have been sent to the world. Instead, calmer heads prevailed and a world weary of war was forced to listen to those who had dragged them to destruction and those who had managed to survive, and testify to, the inhumanity that we as a species are capable of when we allow ourselves to be led by our basest instincts.

In a world where relativism is the new religion, where good and evil are considered antiquated ideas and where the concept of right and wrong is vague and subjective, Nuremberg helped to define what is acceptable conduct in the white heat of war and what is not.

'Nuremberg cannot be forgotten by those who created it. The criminals and their wretched deeds may pass from memory, but the trials we have no right to forget... The great question today is not whether the Nuremberg principles are valid, but whether mankind can live up to them, and whether it can live at all if it fails.'

BRIGADIER-GENERAL TELFORD TAYLOR, FINAL REPORT TO THE ARMY, 1949

Acknowledgements

The author is indebted to the following primary sources for information and for quotes used in this book

Gilbert, G.M., *Nuremberg Diary*, New York: Da Capo, 1995

Neave, Airey, *Nuremberg – A Personal Record of the Trial of the Major Nazi War Criminals*, Coronet, 1978

Selzer, Michael, *Deliverance Day: The Last Hours At Dachau*, London: Sphere, 1980

and to the following website sources:

http://www.adl.org – *for the contemporary views on Nuremberg.*

http://www.eyewitnesstohistory.com – *for the eyewitness account of the executions and Dr Gilbert's notes on the defendants' reactions to sentencing.*

http://www.npr.org – *for the extract from an interview with Sergeant Clancy Sigal.*

http://www.law.umkc.edu/faculty/projects/ftrials/nuremberg/ – *for extracts from trial testimony.*

Picture Credits

Index